Golitsyn Vindicated?: A Second Look at "Splits" in the Communist World During the Cold War

By Nevin Gussack

Executive Summary

Early in the Cold War, American policymakers continuously hoped to weaken the monolithic communist bloc in Europe, Asia, and the rest of the Third World through the policy of differentiation. It was the hope of successive American Administrations to wean selected Marxist-Leninist states away from their alliance with the Soviet Union, capitalize on alleged signs of *"independence"* within the communist bloc, and encourage these countries to accept at least aspects of the capitalist economic system. The ultimate goal of de-linking these nations from the alliance with the Soviet Union was to gradually entice these communist countries into joining the Western camp. Washington's policy of differentiation divided the various communist states into *"good"* (allegedly *"independent"*) and *"bad"* (Soviet satrapies) countries. Virtually all of the Western policymakers involved in the development of the policy of differentiation discounted the notion that the signs of *"independence"* and *"anti-Soviet"* sentiments amongst the communist bloc could in reality be a strategic deception and disinformation operation. Any dissenting voices who called into question Washington's policy of differentiation were pressured to resign or were denied promotions in the foreign policy apparatus and intelligence community. This essay will discuss two well-known examples of nations that were supposedly *"maverick"* communist states who were at odds with the Soviets and friendlier to the Western powers: Romania, and Yugoslavia. It is known that Romania and Yugoslavia specifically implemented policies to deceive the West into believing that they represent a sort of *"independent"* communism. In return, these two Red despotisms received advanced technology and greater trading privileges from capitalist nations, including the United States. The deception would also provide the Western policymakers with a distorted, false perception of the actual unity and strength of the Soviet bloc as arrayed against non-communist interests. The motivations that guided these two communist states to formulate such deception policies and subsequent measures undertaken against the West will be explored in detail throughout this paper. The communist state of Albania will also be covered as a potentially false or vastly overstated *"split"* in the Soviet bloc. In respect to Albania, the trade links with the Soviet bloc were retained and Tirana continued its militantly anti-Western foreign policy which frequently aligned that country with Moscow's interests. At best, one can reasonably conclude after reviewing the evidence, the *"split"* between the Soviet Union and Albania was vastly overstated by many Western scholars and observers. The evidence in respect to Albania is reviewed in this essay.

Albania

After the communist-dominated National Liberation Front under the command of Enver Hoxha conquered Albania and evicted the Germans and their collaborators in 1944, a Red regime was established that was aligned with the Soviet Union and Yugoslavia. By 1946, the communists completed their seizure of power in Albania and wiped out the opposition. The Soviets under Stalin soon transformed Albania into a satellite state that was loyal to the interests of international communism. The Soviets and other Asian and Eastern European communist countries became the dominant military, trade, and political partners of the Hoxha regime. Albanian intelligence personnel were trained in the USSR, while Soviet advisers were stationed in Tirana. The Albanian intelligence service numbered 400 agents and retained residencies in two Western European cities: Paris and Rome. Forty percent of Albanian diplomats at their

French and Italian missions were spies. Albanian agents also operated from embassies in Ankara, East Berlin, Rome, Paris, and Vienna.[1]

Even after the *"split"* of 1960, the Albanians continued to spy on the NATO countries. The Albanian Sigurimi retained a Directorate in the Ministry of Foreign Affairs which placed agents in the diplomatic service of embassies abroad. Sigurimi agents doubled as welcome committees at Albanian border posts, escorts that met foreign (e.g. Greek) tour groups, hotel employees, waiters, and drivers who served foreign visitors. For example, a First Secretary in the embassy in Greece doubled as the Sigurimi agents Harila Kola and Consul Nikola Ziou. Notebooks of Kola's contained classified data and lists of Greeks favorably disposed towards Albania.[2]

The organizational model of the Sigurimi was based on that of the Soviet KGB throughout the period of communist rule in Albania. The Sigurimi maintained agents that were active in Albania's Ministry for Foreign Trade, diplomatic-consular missions, the Ministry of Transportation, and state-owned enterprises such as Transshigip. In reality, assistant truck drivers for Transshigip were Sigurimi agents who engaged in intelligence-reconnaissance work. Other nests of Sigurimi agents were Albturist, the University of Tirana, and the merchant marine. The common feature of all of these state institutions was the fact that all of them maintained connections with visiting foreigners or were engaged in dispatching delegations to other countries. The State Security, Passport and Visa Services, and the Services to Foreign Diplomatic Personnel were all actively involved in controlling and recruiting foreigners. Albturist was completely controlled by the Sigurimi's State Security Department. Sigurimi agents that infiltrated Albturist its director, hotel waiters, cooks, valets, tour guides, and drivers that served foreigners at hotels.[3] The Sigurimi also assassinated anti-communist opponents in exile. This was another trademark of the standard KGB practice of silencing troublesome dissidents residing abroad. For example, the Albanian émigré, Bilal Xhaferri, was politically active and was assassinated in Chicago by the Sigurimi in 1987.[4]

Even around the time of the actual split of 1960 between Soviet dictator Khrushchev and Albanian ruler Hoxha, Moscow continued to maintain a strong presence in Albania. As of mid-1960, it was reported that Albania turned over Sazani Island in the Straits of Oltranto for a Soviet submarine base. Albania exported the vast majority of its products to the Soviet Union, Poland, and Czechoslovakia at low prices. Albanian and Soviet bloc vessels would circumnavigate Europe to ship these products.[5]

The Albanians also supported the efforts of foreign communist terrorists to overthrow governments as far back as the late 1940s. For example, in 1948-1949, Soviet shipments of armaments and food destined for the Greek Communist rebels were received at Albanian ports.[6]

---

[1] USAREUR Intelligence Estimate – 1961 January 1965 US National Archives, Records of the Army Staff Accessed Accessed From:
http://www.php.isn.ethz.ch/collections/colltopic.cfm?lng=en&id=18700&navinfo=14968
[2] Kasimatis, P. "Albanian Agents' Activities in Athens" I Vradyni Tis Kyriakis March 16, 1986
[3] "Organization, Activities of Sigurimi" Narodna Armija March 22, 1990
[4] Trifon Xhagjika, Gazmend Elezi, Namik Mane, Bilal Xhaferri, Ismail Kadare "Albanian Poems of Dissidence" Accessed From: http://www.beyond-the-pale.co.uk/albanian7.htm
[5] Pipa, Arshi. Albanian Stalinism (Eastern European Monographs, 1990) pages 17-18.
[6] Norman, Daniel ""Albania: A Communist Colony" Problems of Communism March 1956 pages 36-37.

The available declassified communist documents clearly highlighted existing tensions between the USSR and Albania. Surprisingly, however, there were strong indications that if a conflict between NATO and the communist world flared up, Albania would join with the Soviets and their European allies. The documents also indicated that Albania's differences with Moscow did not translate into blanket hostility. In fact, Albania and the USSR were quite willing to continue collaboration. Thus, the documents pointed to the fact that the *"split"* between Moscow and Tirana was far from complete and irreversible. In the case of the Albanian-Soviet *"split,"* doctrinal quarrels that were placed in a temporary hiatus if the common interests of global communism dictated the necessity of unity. In 1961, Chinese Foreign Minister Zhou En Lai and Albanian Ambassador Reis Malile held a meeting, where it was noted: *"The Albanian comrades are on the side of good relations (with the Soviet Union); **a softening would be a good thing. It would be such from the position of its necessity for the common struggle against imperialism**, but not in the interest of the strengthening of Khrushchev's position."*[7]

In January 1961, the Albanian Ambassador to China noted to Foreign Minister Zhou En Lai that *"In the socialist camp there have been countries which lie close to imperialism: Korea, Vietnam, Albania, Czechoslovakia and Eastern Germany. Germany does not behave well towards you and us, **but were they to go to war with Western Germany, we would help them**. Tomorrow the (East) German delegation is coming here."*[8]

In 1961, Enver Hoxha discussed his views regarding the Soviet Union with high level Chinese Communist Party official Li Xiannian: *"We, clearly and in an amicable way, told them our views on how our party sees the sacred friendship with the Soviet Union and Lenin's communist party and that our congress attested to this. We told them exactly where our party stands on this issue. We said how our people and party love and will sincerely love the Soviet Union, that we would never wish evil on the Soviet Union, because whoever does that, is wishing evil upon their own people. **We also told them that should something happen to the Soviet Union, the Albanians would be the first to jump to its defense**. We reiterated that those are just not words, but that we have shown in practice and will always prove this in any situation that requires it... Our friendship with the Soviet Union is not simply symbolic. This friendship we must temper in close cooperation with each other, but always the Marxist-Leninist way."*[9]

An interesting quasi-admission cropped up in the text of a Yugoslav news agency report in regard to the 1981 Congress of the Albanian Party of Labor (Communist Party). The text of the report cryptically implied that the Vietnamese delegation to the Albanian Party of Labor Congress represented the interests of the Soviet Union. If the *"split"* of 1960 between the USSR and Albania was a deception, Moscow could have delegated to the pliant Hanoi regime the task of transmitting Soviet *"advice"* to the Tirana regime. North Vietnam (later Vietnam) was a close ally of both Albania and the Soviet Union and the above-mentioned theory should not be dismissed completely out of hand. A Yugoslav report which covered the 1981 Congress of the Albanian Party of Labor noted that: *"...it is known that Albania unreservedly supports*

[7] "Information on the Meeting with Comrade Zhou Enlai" August 21, 1961 Accessed From: http://digitalarchive.wilsoncenter.org/document/110802
[8] "Memorandum of Conversation with Comrade Zhou Enlai, 18 January 1961" Accessed From: http://www.wilsoncenter.org/sites/default/files/CWIHPBulletin16_p3.pdf
[9] "Report on the Second Meeting with the CCP Delegation to the Fourth Congress of the Albanian Labor Party, 25 February 1961" Accessed From: http://www.wilsoncenter.org/sites/default/files/CWIHPBulletin16_p3.pdf

*Vietnamese intervention in Cambodia and all Vietnamese evaluations of the PRC...**Nor is it clear, although there are many reasons why one should think about it, whether the Vietnamese delegation at the Eighth AWP[10] Congress represented itself alone or whether, perhaps, it represented someone else too**.*"[11]

Even in the early days of the *"split,"* relations between Albania and the Soviet bloc continued relatively unabated. This was all the more surprising considering some of the nasty rhetoric and accusations that were exchanged between the tyrants of Tirana and Moscow. In 1960 and 1961, the Albanians participated in both Comecon and Warsaw Pact meetings. The Albanians also sent a delegation to the plenary session of Comecon in Moscow in September 1961. Hoxha signed the Manifesto of the 81st Soviet Communist Party Congress in November 1960. The Albanians issued a special resolution stating that the Communist Party of the Soviet Union was *"the most experienced and competent body of the international communist movement...the hopes of the imperialists, headed by the USA, to split the communist camp are doomed to failure."* Perhaps, this was a message to the West that the *"split"* was either a deception or a disagreement that could be healed very quickly if the needs of proletarian solidarity dictated. Hoxha's report to the Fourth Congress of the Albanian Party of Labor in February 1961 attacked the United States and NATO and praised the USSR, Red China, and the decisions of the 81st Congress of the Communist Party of the Soviet Union. Hoxha's report also recognized the *"general collaboration"* between the USSR and Albania. Albania sent a delegation to the Soviet front World Federation of Trade Unions (WFTU) meeting in Moscow in December 1961.[12] Even at the end of the early 1960s, trade and international exchanges continued between the two countries. In 1962, Poland and Albania signed a trade agreement. Poland was to ship machinery, coke, rolled products, and textiles to Albania.[13] In 1962, East German and Czechoslovak engineers reportedly still worked in Albania, despite the *"split"* with Moscow.[14] In 1963, a delegation from Albania visited the Soviet Union to participate in a conference of the Chemical, Oil, and Allied Industries Workers International in Moscow.[15]

Despite the official severance of relations with Moscow, Albania continued its trade relations with the Soviet satrapies in Eastern Europe. Defecting KGB Major Anatoli Golitsyn observed that *"no economic pressure was brought to bear on Albania by the rest of the bloc. Albanian trade representatives stayed on in Czechoslovakia, East Germany, and Hungary despite criticism of Albania by the party leaders in those countries. In 1962 Poland, Hungary, Bulgaria, Czechoslovakia, and East Germany all signed trade agreements with Albania. After the split, as before, 90 percent of Albania's trade was with other communist countries. The main difference was that China replaced the Soviet Union as Albania's principal supplier."*[16] Since

---

[10] Acronym for Albanian Workers Party, which was another name of the Albanian Party of Labor.
[11] "The Vietnamese Delegation at the AWP Congress: Yugoslav Comment" BBC Summary of World Broadcasts November 18, 1981
[12] Golitsyn, Anatoli. New Lies for Old (Clarion House: Atlanta GA 1984) Accessed From: http://www.spiritoftruth.org/newlies4old.pdf
[13] "Albania Trade with Poland Set" New York Times January 21, 1962 page 26.
[14] "Albanians Hopeful on Help From Bonn" New York Times June 5, 1962 page 5.
[15] "Albanian Mission Arrives in Moscow" New York Times May 21, 1963 page 5.
[16] Golitsyn, Anatoli. New Lies for Old (Clarion House: Atlanta GA 1984) Accessed From: http://www.spiritoftruth.org/newlies4old.pdf

Moscow controlled many of the satellites, the logical step for them would be to cut off trade and relations with Albania. This alone should cause historians to reexamine the nature of the Soviet-Albanian *"split."*

Albania: A Country Study noted that: *"Trade with the Eastern bloc nations increased after Albania broke with China. Generally, Albania supplied its communist-world trading partners with metal ores and agricultural products; it imported machinery, transportation equipment, and some consumer goods. The Albanians obtained rolled steel and coking coal from Poland, pumps from Hungary, trucks and tires from Czechoslovakia, sheet steel from Bulgaria, and textile machinery and fertilizers from East Germany."* It was also reported that Albania had a small amount of trade with Cuba and North Korea.[17]

As of 1985, five foreign airlines flew into Rinas Airport in Tirana. Many of these airlines belonged to Soviet bloc governments. These airlines were Olympic (Greece), Interflug (East Germany), Malev (Hungary), Tarom (Romania), and JAT (Yugoslavia).[18]

Despite angry outpourings against the USSR in the Albanian government press, NATO governments and the United States received an equal, if not larger, amount of abuse and vituperative attacks. Soviet allies were officially endorsed by the Albanian press. As of 1987, foreign movies shown on Albanian television included Soviet films and American films with an antiwar tone.[19] A guide for the official tourist agency Albturist noted to a foreign journalist in November 1989 that *"Why does Albania hate the United States? He replied that the United States is guilty of interventionist policies in Cuba, Chile, Nicaragua and other countries."*[20] In June 1975, Zeri-i-Popullit noted that NATO exercises were *"taking place within the framework of the aggressive policy and escalation of military preparations of US imperialism and its efforts to further strengthen the aggressive NATO pact."*[21]

Tirana also heaped abuse on the independent trade union in Poland called Solidarity. The non-co-opted elements of Solidarity (particularly Fighting Solidarity) fought the ruling communists in Warsaw with strikes, demonstrations, and activism. One visiting communist Hungarian engineer, who was lodged at the luxury Dajti Hotel, reportedly read through the official Albanian publication titled Counter-Revolution Within Counter-Revolution in Poland. This publication criticized the Polish Solidarity labor movement.[22]

In October 1981, the Albanian Trade Union newspaper made the obligatory condemnation of the ruling communists in Poland and equally flayed the Solidarity movement. Arguably, such attacks could have only served Soviet and Warsaw Pact interests. After all, the Poles maintained sizable trade relations with Albania. Hence, Tirana did not despise the ruling Polish Communists enough to sever all relations. The Albanian Trade Union newspaper noted that *"The rottenness of the present social system in Poland has led to the further aggravation of the class struggle, between the Polish proletariat and the new Polish revisionist bourgeoisie. This dissatisfaction of the broad working masses is made use of by the counter-revolutionary*

---

[17] "Albania: A Country Study" Accessed From: http://lcweb2.loc.gov/frd/cs/altoc.html

[18] Lendvai, Paul. "Traveler in Albania" Encounter Magazine May 1985 page 62.

[19] Stokes, Lee. "A rare view of mysterious Albania: part two of three parts; Isolated Albanians live simple life" United Press International April 20, 1987

[20] Howe, Marvine. "Clamor in the East: Island in the Balkans" New York Times November 13, 1989 page 13.

[21] "A New Demonstration of Gunboat Policy" Zeri-i-Popullit June 21, 1975

[22] Lendvai, Paul. "Traveler in Albania" May 1985 Encounter Magazine page 71.

forces, the Catholic clergy, international imperialism. These forces are deceiving the working masses by means of Solidarity and under the veil of the struggle against the anti-worker policy of the Polish revisionist leadership...The slogan of 'independent trade unions' has always been a mask to precisely hide their dependence on the political parties. There has not been and there cannot be apoliticism in the trade union movement. The problem lies: whose interests do the trade union fight for, for the interests of the working class or for those of the bourgeoisie? The more so Solidarity could not be an exception to this. Although dressed in the workers' overalls it came out openly as a representative of reaction and close ally of Vatican and world imperialism...The present strikes in Poland do not lead to the intensification of the revolutionary movement of the working class, they are led by the agents of the bourgeoisie as Lech Walesa and ilk, they play the game of counterrevolutionary forces..."[23]

Even after 1960, NATO installations and personnel were still targeted by agents of the Albanian intelligence service. The Military Intelligence Directorate of the Albanian Armed Forces included NATO countries as targets for their SIGINT and HUMINT operations.[24] Italy expelled Albanian diplomat Koco Kallco in 1962 for spying and stealing Italian military secrets.[25]

There was at least one piece of evidence which pointed to the fact that Albanian agents were also trained in Soviet client states after the "*split*" of 1960. The Samoy School in communist Laos was used to train foreign agents between 1980 and 1988. The Samoy School trained students from Cuba, Bulgaria, Albania, Romania, and East Germany on how to pose as Americans while on intelligence missions. Four captured US Air Force officers served as instructors at the Samoy School.[26]

It also appeared that Albania maintained close military relations with the Soviet satellite of Vietnam. Perhaps Moscow tasked Vietnam with the job of assisting Albania with basic training, the provision of light weapons, and spare parts for Tirana's armed forces. In December 1976, Le Ngoc Thanh, the Charge D'Affairs of Vietnam in Albania hosted a viewing of propaganda films celebrating the 32nd anniversary of the founding of the Vietnamese People's Army. He met with the Deputy Minister of Trade and Deputy Minister of Foreign Affairs of Albania.[27] In December 1983, the Vietnamese Ambassador to Albania held Army Day receptions which were attended by Albanian officials in charge of the armed forces, foreign trade, and international relations and solidarity.[28] Perhaps these meetings served as covers for the

---

[23] "Albanian Trade Union Paper Comments on Poland" Albanian Telegraph Agency October 5, 1981

[24] Bala, Eduart. Intelligence Reform in Albania March 2008 Accessed From: http://www.dtic.mil/docs/citations/ADA479813

[25] "Italy Ousts Albanian" New York Times February 14, 1962 page 16.

[26] "Media Miss Another Big Story" Accuracy In Media Report August A 1994 Accessed From: http://www.aim.org/publications/aim_report/1994/08a.html

[27] "Briefs: Vietnamese Army Anniversary" Tirana Domestic Service December 22, 1976

[28] "Army Day reception at Vietnamese Embassy in Tirana" Albanian Telegraph Agency December 31, 1983 and "Deputy Defence Minister Jace Lula at Vietnamese Embassy reception" Albanian Telegraph Agency December 30, 1982

provisioning of Soviet weapons to Albania. Unbelievably, an unconfirmed report stated that East Germany supplied 6 MIG-23 fighter planes to the Albanian Air Force in the early 1980s.[29]

There was also evidence that Moscow established Albania as an *"independent"* drug peddler in the Soviet *"Red Cocaine"* operation to corrupt and demoralize the West. This would also give Moscow and Albania further grounds for plausible denial in respect to continued Western suspicions of continued collaboration, even after the *"split"* of 1960. According to defecting Czech Major General Jan Sejna, *"Albania had asked to participate (in the Soviet and Warsaw Pact drug operation), emphasizing its strong intelligence network in the Balkans and the Middle East. But rather than bring Albania into the operation, the Soviets decided to provide Albania with the money to purchase the necessary equipment, so that Albania could proceed as an 'independent' drug promoter."*[30] Albania served as a port and base for morphine trafficking by the Union Corse and Marseilles illicit refiners of opium and morphine.[31]

The Soviets also continued to spout lofty phrases about *"friendship"* with Albania during the years of the *"split."* This is strange, in light of the very real attacks that characterized the genuine *"split"* between Yugoslavia and the USSR in the period 1948 to 1953. There were no professions of friendship between Yugoslavia and the USSR during much of this time period. Why then would there be continued professions of friendship between the USSR and Albania? In 1963, the Soviets considered Albania a member of the *"socialist camp"* despite the activities of the *"splitting activities"* of its leaders and the Soviets reportedly had taken unspecified steps to prevent Albania's *"estrangement from the Socialist family."*[32]

Radio Moscow noted in November 1964 that *"The Soviet Union and the other socialist states have helped Albania to assume its place in the international arena and to increase its influence...Soviet citizens wholeheartedly wish the workers of the Albanian People's Republic new successes."*[33]

In November 1964, Izvestia noted on the 20th anniversary of the communist takeover of Albania that Soviet relations with Albania were based on *"the principles of proletarian internationalism, equality and respect for national independence, non-interference in internal affairs and close cooperation and mutual assistance."*[34]

V. Dobrov noted in Pravda in November 1969 that the *"normalization of Soviet Albanian relations on the basis of equality, mutual respect and noninterference in each other's affairs."* The Supreme Soviet also sent Albania a message that stated *"The Soviet Union has been invariably coming out for the development of cooperation and friendship with the People's Republic of Albania."* Albanian folk music was also played on Moscow radio.[35]

In December 1969, Izvestia noted on the 25th anniversary of the communist takeover in Albania that *"The Soviet people express the profound conviction that contrary to intrigues by*

---

[29] "MIG-23 Flogger Versus Western Fighters" X Air Forces Aviation Society Accessed From: http://www.xairforces.net/analyses/mig-23.html

[30] Douglass, Joseph D. Red Cocaine (Edward Harle, Limited, 1999) Accessed From: http://www.usa-anti-communist.net/Perestroika-4books/Douglass_Joseph_Red_Cocaine.pdf

[31] Hoar, William P. "Red Europe" American Opinion July-August 1975 page 100.

[32] "Soviet Union Says Albania Is Still in Socialist Family" New York Times September 8, 1963 page 24.

[33] "Soviet Sends Albania Friendship Message" New York Times November 11, 1964 page 5.

[34] "Soviet Salutes Albania on Liberation Holiday" New York Times November 28, 1964 page 2.

[35] "Friendliness Shown Albania by Soviet" New York Times November 29, 1969 page 30.

hostile forces Soviet-Albanian friendship will ultimately triumph and the People's Republic of Albania will again occupy a worthy place among the ranks of socialist states."[36]

Even the official friendship organizations of the USSR and Albania continued to hold meetings. Izvestia reported that the Soviet-Albanian Friendship Society held its board meeting in Moscow in January 1981, which celebrated the 35th Anniversary of the founding of the Albanian People's Republic.[37]

During the dictatorship of Gorbachev, the Soviets and Albanians officially reconciled, thus healing the *"split."* Official trade relations were also restarted between the Soviets and Albanians. In September 1990, Soviet Deputy Foreign Trade Minister Yevgeniy Osadchuk told TASS that several trade contracts were signed with the Albanian communists. One agreement stipulated that Albania would export to the USSR cigarettes in exchange for chemicals.[38]

In November 1990, Ramiz Alia sent a telegram to Gorbachev, which congratulated him and the Soviet people on the anniversary of the October Revolution. Alia hoped that *"the relations of co-operation between Albania and the USSR would develop in the interests of their two peoples and peace and security in Europe."*[39]

Soviet Deputy Minister of Foreign Economic Relations Ye.I.Osadchuk concluded a trade agreement with Albania in March 1991. This agreement stipulated that the Soviet Union would deliver to Albania coking coals, ferriferous raw materials, ferrous and non-ferrous metallurgical products, timber, mineral fertilizers, spare parts for various machines and equipment, and individual consumer goods. Albania agreed to export to the Soviet Union fresh and canned vegetables and fruit, cognac and wine, tobacco and cigarettes, construction materials, and medicinal herbs.[40]

In April 1991, a delegation of Soviet economic specialists, representatives of the Soviet Ministry for Foreign Economic Relations, Soviet trade enterprises, and factories visited Albania. The Soviets conferred with officials of the Albanian Ministry of Foreign Trade and Economic Cooperation, Albanian businessmen, and a number of institutions and industrial enterprises regarding the modernization of existing Albanian factories.[41]

In June 1991, the Secretariat of the Soviet Communist Party Central Committee congratulated the representatives attending the 10th Congress of the Albanian Party of Labor. Pravda noted that *"positive changes in Soviet-Albanian relations have been regarded with ardent approval in our country...Consistently moving ahead in this cause, we shall jointly get rid of encrustations of the past and open up a prospect of friendly co-operation before the peoples of the Soviet Union and Albania...The Soviet Communist Party, for its part, is prepared to make a contribution to creating a climate of trust and with this end in view establish contacts with the APL*[42] *in forms that will be acceptable and beneficial for the two parties."*[43]

---

[36] "Soviet in Bid to Albania" New York Times December 1, 1969 page 17.

[37] Golitsyn, Anatoli. New Lies for Old (Clarion House: Atlanta GA 1984) Accessed From: http://www.spiritoftruth.org/newlies4old.pdf

[38] "Resumption of Trade Relations with Albania" TASS September 7, 1990

[39] "Albanian greetings to USSR on October Revolution anniversary" BBC Summary of World Broadcasts November 8, 1990

[40] "Resumption of Economic Links with Albania" Izvestiya March 22, 1991

[41] "Soviet economic specialists in Albania" Albanian Telegraph Agency May 6, 1991

[42] The APL was the acronym for the ruling Albanian Party of Labor.

[43] "CPSU Secretariat greets Albanian Labour Party" TASS June 13, 1991

In September 1990, the Albanian communist ruler Ramiz Alia met with the President of Occidental Petroleum, Armand Hammer to discuss *"economic cooperation between the United States of America and Albania, in the oil sector in particular."* The Permanent Representative of Albania at the United Nations Bashkim Pitarka was present at the meeting between Alia and Hammer.[44] It should be noted that Hammer was an American industrialist who was an agent of influence for the Soviet Union since the time of Lenin's rule. Hence, discussions regarding increased Albanian-US trade were conducted with a *bona fide* Soviet agent.

Even when Albania broke off its close relations with Red China in 1978, relations between the two countries were soon quietly reestablished. In 1983, a Chinese delegation from the Ministry of Foreign Economic Relations and Trade visited Albania to restart trade relations with that communist nation. The Chinese discussed with the Albanians spare parts for machinery.[45] Some analysts also reported that China continued to supply Albania with spare parts for their weapons systems in the 1980s.[46] Since 1984, shipping containers from Red China were unloaded at the port of Durres and were believed to contain spare parts for Chinese-made tanks and aircraft in the Albanian Army inventory.[47] When Hoxha died in April 1985, Chinese Premier Li Peng offered condolences to *"Comrade Hoxha"* at the Albanian Embassy in Beijing. Li Peng also extended congratulations to *"Comrade Alia being elected as the first secretary of the Central Committee of the Albanian Worker's Party."*[48] Hence, the Sino-Albanian *"split"* was also healed after bitter, outward condemnation and relations between the two countries resumed under the surface.

Following the example of the Soviet Union and Red China, Albania also supported terrorist movements and communist parties, including ones that were sympathetic to Hoxha's brand of Stalinist Communism. From 1966 to 1970, the Albanian Party of Labor trained and funded foreign guerrilla movements from Asia, Africa, and Latin America. One Italian leftist group requested in May 1969 military training from Albania *"for the triumph of the proletarian revolution."*[49] From 1968 to April 1991, a translator from New Zealand translated Enver Hoxha's works into English. He was paid at least $10,000 by the Albanians. He was paid via the account of the Fund for Solidarity of the Albanian Party of Labor. It was reported that Decision Number 190 of the Central Committee of the Albanian Party of Labor, issued in 1964, had the *"the aim of the creation of this fund was to (further) the interest of the work for the international communist movement, for the combat against imperialism and revisionism and for the propagation of Marxism-Leninism."* From 1964 to 1991, over $3 million was disbursed to

[44] "Alia Meets US Industrialist in New York" ATA September 27, 1990
[45] Oziewicz, Stanley. "Albania, China may reforge ties, renew trade link" The Globe and Mail (Canada) April 20, 1983
[46] "Albania: A Country Study" (Washington: GPO for the Library of Congress, 1994.) Accessed From: http://countrystudies.us/albania/153.htm
[47] "Security Service, Military Strength Described" Belgrade Borba January 15, 1990
[48] Pi Ying-hsien. "PRC/Eastern European Relations and East Europes's Views on China's Economic Reforms" Journal of Social, Political, and Economic Studies Volume 12 1987 pages 157-183.
[49] "Headline: AWP Archives Reported to Reveal Funding of Marxist-Leninist Parties, Terrorists" Radio Tirana May 22, 1993

terrorist, leftist, and communist groups worldwide from the Solidarity Fund.[50] In Italy, funds disbursed to communist and leftist groups were at first paid from the Solidarity Fund to the Albanian Embassy in Italy. Years later, payments were then disbursed from the Solidarity Fund to the Italy-Albania Friendship Association.[51] In January 1967, 19 Indonesian communists traveled to Tirana from Prague, Czechoslovakia for training. This Tirana to Prague trip may also indicate a level of cooperation of Albania with a Soviet satellite even during the *"split."* Such alleged cooperation probably was rooted all in the name of *"international solidarity"* within the communist camp. At the same time, the Communist Party of Sudan received Albanian approval to send to Albania 15 cadres per year for *"military-political training."* During 1968, the Communist Party of Ceylon (Sri Lanka) dispatched three Party members to Albania for military and political training. In 1970, Albania approved ideological and military training for Marxist-Leninist parties Third World countries, such as Ecuador, Brazil, and Peru. These foreign groups received training all the way through 1984.[52] When the Solidarity Fund was created in 1964, it had $11.6 million in cash. Four million dollars was used for extreme left groups in Italy and West Germany. The goal of the plan of the Solidarity Fund was to *"prepare the triumph of the proletarian revolution."* From 1964 to 1970, these foreign leftists and communists trained in Albanian People's Army schools and served for six month terms in the Albanian Army. At least $244,000 dollars was used to fund French Marxist-Leninist groups. The Albanian Defense Ministry provided an additional $200,000 to train foreign terrorists. In 1990, the Solidarity Fund allocated $400,000 dollars for the Albanian Party of Labor to purchase a printing press in Denmark.[53] The Marxist dictator of the Democratic Republic of the Congo (DRC) Laurent Kabila was trained in Albania during the 1960s. This training was financed by the Albanian Party of Labor's Solidarity Fund.[54] In May 1990, an American citizen donated $84 million dollars to the Albanian Party of Labor.[55]

The Albanians also forged close ties with pro-Soviet terror groups and regimes in the Third World. In July 1980, an Albanian communist delegation attended the International Conference on the Crimes of America in Islamic Iran. The Albanian delegation to Iran was led by Professor Sofokli Lazri.[56] Documentaries were aired on Albanian television which praised terrorist groups such as the PLO and ANC.[57] It was also noted that the Albanian communists

---

[50] "Headline: AWP Archives Reported to Reveal Funding of Marxist-Leninist Parties, Terrorists" Radio Tirana May 22, 1993

[51] "Headline: ATA Reports Further Revelations from AWP Archives on Funding for Terrorism" Albanian Telegraph Agency May 24, 1993

[52] Ibid.

[53] "Albania trained foreign terrorists: government official" Agence France Presse April 18, 1995

[54] "Congo leader reportedly educated in Albania" Deutsche Presse-Agentur May 25, 1997

[55] "US resident reportedly donated 84m dollars to AWP in 1990" Albanian Telegraph Agency November 8, 1993

[56] "Albanian condemnation of US 'crimes' in Iran" Albanian Telegraph Agency July 7, 1980

[57] Hogarth, David. "Albania: A Fortress of 'Unshakable Granite'" IPS-Inter Press Service August 3, 1987

supported the Palestine Liberation Army.[58] The Iraqis in the 1970s reportedly hosted Chinese and Albanian advisers that attached to their intelligence service.[59]

In 1981, Albania noted that: *"We note with particular satisfaction the friendly development of the relations of our country with Algeria, Syria, Iraq, Libya, Lebanon, Tunisia, Egypt, and other Arab countries. We desire that these relations should find further concretization and development. Likewise, the PSR of Albania is for friendly relations with the Islamic Republic of Iran and will spare no efforts for their development and strengthening."*[60]

Following the Soviet and Chinese examples, the Albanians were given propaganda support by a number of leftists and progressives in the West. A number of tourist groups, including American citizens, visited Albania by the spring of 1989. Included in these delegations were clergymen who had *"good things to say for the Albanian atheist regime."* Dr. and Mrs. Edwin E. Jacques prefaced their unpublished report dated from November 1986 with *"This report was deliberately kept low key so as to be shared with six Tirana dignitaries with whom we had contact."* The Very Reverend Arthur E. Liolin Chancellor of the Albanian Archdiocese in America toured Albania in July-August 1988 and had only *"lyrical"* praises for the Albanian communists and no criticism of its religious persecution.[61]

The Freeman reported in 1991 that *"as with Ceausescu's Romania, there are plenty of socialists in the West prepared to see no evil in their praise for Albanian socialism. Written while Hoxha still ruled, Albania Defiant by Jan Myrdal and Gun Kessle is an adulatory account of a workers' paradise fighting to retain independence from the alien and corrupting influences of the outside world. Christopher Brown, writing in the supposedly moderate British socialist newspaper Tribune (June 9, 1990), eulogizes the simple life enjoyed by Albanians, freed from the pressures of materialism."*[62]

Romania

Under the rule of Gheorghe Gheorgiu-Dej, the ruling communists undertook a strategic disinformation operation that was coordinated with the USSR. Its strategic goal was to portray Romania as a *"maverick,"* *"independent,"* and *"national-minded"* Marxist-Leninist regime that could cooperate and trade with the West and the United States. By the early 1950s, the Warsaw Pact countries in Eastern Europe retained a poor image in the West and the United States as result of Soviet political controls over the native communist leadership and Moscow's outright military occupation of Hungary, East Germany, and Romania. By launching a disinformation operation to portray Romania as a nation *"independent"* from Moscow's dominance, the communists were convinced that the West and the United States would increase trade with Bucharest. Also, Moscow and the Bloc would derive the strategic advantage of portraying international communism as a less than monolithic force which did not threaten the West. Furthermore, the West and the United States would be influenced by Soviet agents of influence and corporate internationalists to implement the policy of *"differentiation,"* which in turn was

---

[58] Thomson, I.M. "Alien in the land of Zog" Sunday Times June 5, 1988

[59] Deacon, Richard. The Israeli Secret Service (Little, Brown Book Group Limited 1994) pages 200-201.

[60] "On relations with the Arab peoples" BBC Summary of World Broadcasts November 4, 1981

[61] Pipa, Arshi. "Glasnost in Albania" Telos Spring 1989 page 181.

[62] "Albania: Europe's Last Marxist Holdout" The Freeman April 1991 pages 128-131.

based on the combination of Romanian/Soviet disinformation, corporate greed, and the philosophy of globalism and internationalism that was espoused by our diplomats, academics, and politicians. Rodica Eliza Gheorghe reported that *"the Romanian intelligence services leaked the news (of the Soviet troop withdrawal from Romania) to American diplomats, in an attempt to manipulate Washington's view about Moscow's grip on its satellites. Romania was supposed to make the United States believe that the USSR was no longer willing to maintain a strong military presence in South-Eastern Europe. Moreover, since Romania was the only country in the Soviet bloc to obtain such a concession from Moscow, it could attract the attention of the West and thus create the conditions for a denial and deception operation."*[63]

A withdrawal of Soviet troops from Romania was also viewed by Moscow and Bucharest as a tool to deprive Western anti-communists of their charge that Eastern Europe was under the sole control of the USSR. The measure would deprive the anti-communists worldwide of the bogeyman of Red Army domination of Eastern Europe and the *"fear"* of monolithic communism. A disunited bloc would then compel Western governments to reduce their military preparedness and become less vigilant on the intelligence front. In a 1958 letter to Gheorghe Gheorghiu Dej, Soviet dictator Khrushchev noted that ***"We should add that imperialist circles, in order to serve their anti-Soviet propaganda and to slander the Romanian People's Republic, make large use of the fact that Soviet troops are still stationed on your country's territory. The withdrawal of the Soviet troops from the territory of the Romanian People's Republic would be a new palpable and convincing proof of the peace-loving policy of the Soviet Union, of the Romanian People's Republic and of the socialist camp as a whole, of our common tendency to obtain, not by words, but by facts, a relaxation of international tension. Such an act would deprive imperialist circles of one of their significant arguments in favor of their policy of military preparation and would contribute to uniting the forces that pronounce themselves for the safeguarding and consolidation of peace, for peaceful coexistence among states."***[64]

Dej responded to Khrushchev in 1958 by accurately anticipating the results of the strategic withdrawal of Soviet troops from Romania: *"We have no doubt whatsoever that this decision will have a major impact and would be seen by world public opinion as a new palpable contribution of the USSR, of the Romanian People's Republic and of the entire socialist camp, to the strengthening of peace and to détente in international relations."*[65]

---

[63] Rodica Eliza Gheorghe. The Romanian Intelligence Services During the Cold War Georgetown University Washington DC April 16, 2010 Accessed From: http://repository.library.georgetown.edu/bitstream/handle/10822/553496/gheorgheRodica.pdf?sequence=1

[64] "Letter addressed by N.S. Khrushchev, First Secretary of the CC of the CPSU to the CC of the RWP concerning the withdrawal of Soviet troops from the Romanian territory" April 17, 1958 Accessed From: http://www.wilsoncenter.org/index.cfm?topic_id=1409&fuseaction=va2.document&identifier=5034F347-96B6-175C-981BC8FFC1591CD5&sort=Collection&item=Romania%20in%20the%20Cold%20War

[65] "Letter of reply, from Gheorghe Gheorgiu-Dej, First Secretary of the CC of the RWP expressing agreement to the proposal made by the Soviet Union to withdraw its troops from Romania" April 23, 1958 Accessed From: http://www.wilsoncenter.org/index.cfm?topic_id=1409&fuseaction=va2.document&identifier=5

Rodica Eliza Gheorghe reported that *"continuing the duplicitous policy of independence inaugurated in 1958, in April 1964 the Romanian Workers Party (RWP) launched its most virulent attack to date against the Soviet Union. Known as the 'April Theses,' the declaration issued by the RWP, blamed Moscow for the crisis of the international communist movement and called for the removal of KGB officers from the ranks of the Romanian intelligence services, in particular the Securitate. Soviet sources indicate that the Romanians coordinated with the Soviets before issuing the declaration. In an interview with Romanian historian Armand Gosu, Vladimir Bukovsky, the famous Russian dissident, declared that he saw the document in the Soviet Archives after the collapse of the Soviet Union, which summarizes the discussions between the leadership of the Romanian Workers Party and the leadership of the Communist Party of the Soviet Union."[66]*

These plans culminated in the *"removal"* of Soviet troops in Romania. Defecting Romanian foreign intelligence (DIE) General Ion Pacepa recalled being told by Ceausescu that he allegedly ordered the old-line Romanian Communist Emil Bodnaras to request Khrushchev to withdraw Soviet troops from Romania *"saying that it would help neutralize Western propaganda claims that the Romanian government would not be able to remain in power without Soviet bayonets."* Pacepa reported that it was actually Gheorghe Gheorgiu-Dej who negotiated with Khrushchev to withdraw Soviet troops from Romania.[67]

The plan to increase the scope of Romanian disinformation directed at Western and American policymakers received a huge push under the rule of Nicolae Ceausescu. On February 22, 1972, Nicolae Ceausescu spoke to a meeting of high ranking Securitate officers where he outlined the long-range Romanian disinformation program called Operation Horizon: *"Our experience shows that today the West is commendably eager to encourage the slightest sign of independence within the Soviet bloc. Let's take advantage of their eagerness. We must make cleverness our national trait...Stop showing a sullen frowning face and clenched fist to the West. Start making it feel compassion for us and you'll see how fast Western boycotts change into magnanimity. Let's present Romania as a Latin island in the Slavic sea...Our millennia old traditions of independence are now up against Moscow's political centrism...A pawn between two superpowers..."* Pacepa noted that Ceausescu tasked the Romanian foreign intelligence service (DIE) with the job of *"carefully plant(ing) little hints of independence without affecting the fundamentals of communism-and then hammer away at them in order to stir up the West's sympathy for Romania and gain its political and economic assistance."* Ceausescu was committed to the cause of unified international communism: *"Romania should make a substantial increase in its contribution to the defense not only of the Warsaw Pact but also of Peking and the whole communist world."[68]* Ceausescu clearly comprehended that one of the most effective tools in the communist arsenal were influence operations (a.k.a. disinformation): *"For me, influence comes first. I firmly believe that it can open the tightest doors, including*

034F395-96B6-175C-9BDD021B060452BF&sort=Collection&item=Romania%20in%20the%20Cold%20War
[66] Rodica Eliza Gheorghe. The Romanian Intelligence Services During the Cold War Georgetown University Washington DC April 16, 2010 Accessed From: http://repository.library.georgetown.edu/bitstream/handle/10822/553496/gheorgheRodica.pdf?sequence=1
[67] Pacepa. Ion. Red Horizons (Regnery Washington DC 1990) page 256.
[68] Ibid, page 8.

technological ones. If Moscow gets a younger man in the Kremlin after the Bear croaks, he'll do exactly as I do. I'll lay you a hundred and one on that."[69]

During the period of *"independence"* from Moscow, the Soviets and Romanians cooperated on joint projects related to the funneling of dual use, war-related technologies to the KGB and mutual collaboration in supporting the *"peace"* movement in the West as a means of disarming NATO and the United States. During a visit to a Soviet secret city, Leonid Brezhnev noted to Ceausescu that *"now when our nuclear capability can destroy the Western Hemisphere many times over, our first priority is to build rockets able to reach American rockets even before they are launched…The most modern microelectronics is what we need for that."* Romania had that technology transferred to Moscow for military purposes. As a result, Brezhnev praised Ceausescu for penetrating Texas Instruments.[70] Brezhnev reportedly sent Minister of the Interior Nikolay Shchelokov to request from Ceausescu *"comradely assistance"* in supporting the *"nuclear freezers"* and the international peace movement as *"ways to disarm the West."*[71]

Pacepa noted that the Warsaw Pact (including Romania) also cooperated in efforts to the fool the Western Left and the *"peace"* movements by publicizing false statistics on the defense budgets of the European Communist countries: *"Within the Warsaw Pact the published defense figures are coordinated by the Kremlin and formally approved by the politburo of each member country. These figures which are far from the real ones, have only propaganda and disinformation value. They are basically intended to provide political meat for non-ruling communist parties in the West and for international peace movements as well as to shield the true defense effort from Western analysis. The real, unpublished defense budget has the highest possible security classification and only a handful of people have the right to know it in its entirety."*[72]

Ceausescu and Yugoslav dictator Marshal Josip Broz Tito specifically used their public images of *"independence"* to harness the greed and short-sightedness of Western businessmen into providing military-related and industrial technologies to their respective countries. Such a strategy was to be kept in absolute secret from the naïve or corrupt Western and American businessmen and political leaders. In a meeting with Tito, Ceausescu noted that the DIE mission was *"to build communism with capitalism's political help, money, and technology through influence operations."* Tito noted that *"We wouldn't be able to get anything from the West by riding on Moscow's coattails and without Western money and technology there wouldn't be any communist society in our countries. That's why we should have our own way of dealing with capitalism."* Ceausescu noted in response *"Letting the West believe that we're different, that we don't want its scalp."* Tito responded *"They call it 'Tito's Triangle.' I set up three basic guidelines: friendly smile toward the West, maximum take from it, and no contamination from capitalism…But that's not something we want to talk about out loud-not here on this yacht and not even in our deepest sleep. Let our men work together. They know what we need and they can keep their mouths shut."*[73]

Former American Ambassador to Romania David Funderburk recalled *"a telling conversation (that) took place some years ago in the wake of the defection of a foreign trade*

---

[69] Ibid, page 226.

[70] Ibid, page 41.

[71] Ibid, page 46.

[72] Ibid, page 207.

[73] Ibid, pages 349-350.

minister from Romania. When Americans asked the Romanian defector if it was not a US-Western plan to lend money to Romania to make Bucharest more dependent on and tied to the West (thus helping separate the Romanian Communists from Moscow), the answer was not publicized. It did not fit US policy theories. In the conversation the Romanian said matter of factly that he spent considerable time each week coordinating with the Soviets plans to get more money in the form of loans, credits, grants, and even technology from the US and the West."[74] In other words, the Romanians and the Soviets colluded with each other to extract hard currency loans from Western and American banks and governments to help finance communism.

Even well into the 1980s, Romania continued to create carefully crafted disinformation ploys to prove its *bona fides* as an *"independent"* communist country. Such stances were conjured up in coordination with the Soviets. Funderburk reported that "*A Romanian official at some risk told me that the Romanians had asked the Soviets several months earlier whether Romania should go to the Olympics and thus keep intact its image of 'independence.' I reported this private conversation to the State Department but to no avail because it ran counter to the State line.*"[75]

Soviet KGB defector Major Anatoli Golitsyn pointed out the hidden strings that secretly comprised the Romanian-Soviet relationship and the superficial disinformation ploy of Bucharest's *"independence"*: "*The surest signs of disinformation in action are to be seen in the contrast between the well-advertised, superficial Romanian disagreements with Comecon and the binding effect of her continued membership in the organization and her participation, for example, in joint energy projects in Eastern Europe. Similarly, occasional well-publicized Romanian refusals to participate in military exercises should blind no one to the fact that Romania remains a member of the Warsaw Pact. The Romanians' ostensible rejection of Soviet influence must be seen alongside the continuing exchanges of friendly visits between the Soviet and Romanian leaders and the award to Ceausescu of an Order of Lenin in Moscow in January 1978.*"[76]

Golitsyn also wrote that "*In the case of Romania, some of Ceausescu's many visits to the Soviet Union have been well publicized. Western commentators, under the influence of disinformation, have almost always assumed that these visits were made in an attempt to resolve the differences between the Soviet and Romanian leaders. But the evidence of Romania's participation in Warsaw Pact, Comecon, Crimean, and other multilateral and bilateral meetings within the bloc far outweighs the occasional evidence of her nonparticipation and is inconsistent with the existence of serious differences. It points to the conclusion that, when Ceausescu met Brezhnev, it was not to be reprimanded by him, but to work out in practical terms how the fiction of Romanian independence could best be maintained and exploited in the interests of long-range policy.*"[77]

In October 1970, Ceausescu signed an agreement with the USSR that strengthened the role of the Securitate (domestic secret police of Romania) in ensuring peace in the Balkans. Antal also wrote that "*On the international stage Ceausescu struck an anti-Soviet attitude. That made a good impression on the West. At home hidden pipes under the sea and long trains of*

---

[74] Funderburk, David M. Pinstripes and Reds (Selous Foundation Press, 1987) page 54.
[75] Ibid, page 110.
[76] Golitsyn, Anatoli. New Lies for Old (Clarion House: Atlanta GA 1984) Accessed From http://www.spiritoftruth.org/newlies4old.pdf
[77] Ibid.

tankers were secretly carrying our oil to the big, bottomless belly of the Soviet Empire. That kept the Russians happy. Let this little man talk against us. It's good for the West to believe that we have a voice of discontent within our communist puppet satellites."[78]

Even in the last months of Ceausescu's rule, Romania's alliance with the Soviet bloc was enhanced. Fearful that the Gorbachev deception would create a chain of events that would spin out of control, Ceausescu remained retrenched in his brand of hard-line Stalinist communism. In October 1989, defecting Romanian intelligence officer Liviu Turcu reported that Ceausescu engaged in *"propaganda activities designed to convince both the West and the East that his regime is more stable than ever, despite evidence to the contrary; a flirtation with Soviet President Mikhail Gorbachev in ways intended to keep Romania away from the Gorbachev agenda; an attempt to consolidate under his control a bizarre axis made up of the conservative leaders of East Germany and Czechoslovakia that can be transformed into an anti-reformist front against heretics seeking to revise Marxist dogma; and a scheme to force Western countries to recognize his regime as an integral, if unwanted, partner in world affairs."*[79]

Despite the détente and friendly relations with President Nixon, Ceausescu still believed that the United States and its leaders remained the ultimate class enemy of all communists. A declassified document from the Romanian Communist Party Executive Committee which was dated from August 1969 reported that Comrade Gheorghe Stoica stated *"I fully agree with the tone set by these discussions and I think we can congratulate Comrade Ceausescu and Comrade Maurer who achieved these results. **Of course, imperialism remains imperialism**.*"[80] This statement was made in reference to President Nixon's visit to Bucharest. Anti-Americanism was prolific on the Romanian home front. Romanian TV, radio, newspapers, books, and magazines reflected an anti-capitalist, atheist, anti-NATO, and anti-US line. Romanian students were taught that the West and the United States in particular were the enemies of communism.[81]

Ceausescu clearly remained loyal to the concept of an alliance of the Eastern Bloc against NATO and the United States. He was also convinced that the Warsaw Pact could dissolve if Europe was sufficiently neutralized. Ceausescu also noted: *"I would like to stress that even after the Warsaw Pact's dissolution we believe that the socialist countries should continue to cooperate and to act in concert, preserve cooperation and joint action among ourselves, including in military terms. This is necessary."*[82]

Ceausescu also admitted that the current ploy of disarmament and *"peace"* did not mean the slackening off of its military buildup of the Bloc countries, including Romania. In May 1989, Ceausescu stated at a meeting of the Defense Council of the Socialist Republic of Romania that

[78] Antal, Dan. Out of Romania (Faber & Faber, 1995) page 125.
[79] Turcu, Liviu. "An offensive born of desperation" The Washington Times October 11, 1989 page F4.
[80] Minutes of the Meeting of the RCP CC Executive Committee Regarding US President Richard Nixon's Visit to Romania (2-3 August), and the Discussions that Took Place on that Occasion, 4 August 1969 Accessed From:
http://www.wilsoncenter.org/sites/default/files/CWIHPBulletin16_p4.pdf
[81] Funderburk, David M. Pinstripes and Reds (Selous Foundation Press, 1987) pages 72-73.
[82] Speech by the General Secretary of the Romanian Communist Party and President of the Socialist Republic of Romania, Comrade Nicolae Ceauşescu at the Meeting of the PCC of the Warsaw Treaty Member-States Bucharest, 7-8 July 1989 Accessed From:
http://www.php.isn.ethz.ch/collections/colltopic.cfm?lng=en&id=19041&navinfo=14465

*"**The fact must be well understood that the policy of disarmament and peace of our party and state does not mean a weakening of the combat capability; as long as imperialism still exists, as long as a policy of force is resorted to, until the elimination of nuclear weapons and of other weapons of mass destruction is reached, and a substantial reduction of conventional armament is made, the danger of a war breaking out still exists. But even afterwards, with diminished effectives and armament, it will be all the more necessary for the army and the combat units to be better trained and better disciplined in order for them to be able to fulfill their mission**. War will take a long time to completely disappear from the life of humankind, and in the activity that we are carrying out no illusion should be created–and if such an illusion happens to arise, it has to be suppressed right away–that a danger of war no longer exists, and we can relax order and scale down military combat training."*[83]*

Ceausescu noted *"Therefore, I once again turn to the participants of this conference with a call to strengthen our cooperation in resolving all these problems. We must improve the work of the Warsaw Treaty. Many proposals have been put forward. Of course, we are in favor of dissolving this Treaty, but as long as it exists, it must work under good conditions."*[84]

Despite popular perceptions, Romanian officers and troops continued to participate in Warsaw Pact military maneuvers, with an eye to defeating Western imperialism and NATO. In 1982, Romanian troops directly participated directly in Warsaw Pact exercises in Bulgaria.[85] Romanian officers participated in Shield-84 Warsaw Pact exercises.[86] A Vienna-based Western expert noted in 1984 that *"Romania is much more involved in the Warsaw Pact than it would like the world to think."* A Western diplomat noted: *"Romania is an integrated member of the Warsaw Pact, with many contacts. There have been signs of increased cooperation over the past two years, coincident with an increase of trade with the Soviet Union."*[87] In a 1986 interview, Colonel-General Vasile Milea noted that *"Romania is participating in the Warsaw Pact which as is well known was created in order to defend against an imperialistic attack on Europe."* It was also noted that *"in keeping with its international obligations the Romanian Army will always perform its defensive tasks together with friendly armies and against an imperialist attack."*[88]

The Ceausescu regime allowed Soviet troops to pass through Romania. Funderburk noted *"During my stay in Bucharest one American official accidentally stumbled on a large Soviet*

---

[83] "Stenographic transcript of the meeting of the Defense Council of the Socialist Republic of Romania" May 31, 1989 Accessed From: http://www.wilsoncenter.org/index.cfm?topic_id=1409&fuseaction=va2.document&iden tifier=5034F366-96B6-175C-903E61803DBCB0EE&sort=Collection&item=Romania%20in%20t he%20Cold%20War

[84] Speech by the General Secretary of the Romanian Communist Party and President of the Socialist Republic of Romania, Comrade Nicolae Ceauşescu at the Meeting of the PCC of the Warsaw Treaty Member-States Bucharest, 7-8 July 1989 Accessed From: http://www.php.isn.ethz.ch/collections/colltopic.cfm?lng=en&id=19041&navinfo=14465

[85] "The Shield-82 exercises" BBC Summary of World Broadcasts September 25, 1982

[86] "International News" Associated Press September 15, 1984

[87] "Military exercises apparently first in Romania in more than a decade" United Press International February 22, 1984

[88] Lazanski, Miroslav. "Romanian Initiative: A Referendum on Insubordination" DANAS October 28, 1986

convoy crossing Romanian territory. He fell in line and observed at length the Soviet troop transit." Soviet troops transited Romania when traveling from Soviet Moldovia and Bulgaria. In a July 1984, Ceausescu admitted in an interview to John Wallach that Warsaw Pact troops in transit to exercises in Bulgaria transited Romania. Ceausescu also admitted that Romania participated in Warsaw Pact exercises.[89]

On the home front, Romania prepared for war and even had some ambitions of its own to be a leader of international communism in the aftermath of a Third World War. Romanian tunnels in Bucharest were built to withstand nuclear weapons; rooms were stocked with canned and frozen delicacies; armories stored missiles; and communications centers were equipped with modern technology. Ceausescu felt that a nuclear war was imminent and after the radiation levels settled, Ceausescu and his troops planned to emerge and conquer a ruined world. Underground hangers stored planes to transport goods in this ruined world, while oil was stored in empty oil fields of Ploesti. The tunnels had giant refrigerators that stored foods, meats, quality shoes and clothes, comfortable dorms, modern electronics and monitoring equipment, computers, weapons, bombs, and germ warfare shells.[90]

The Romanian communist theoreticians also appeared to have developed strategies to advance communism in Western Europe. A Romanian professor pointed out that *"in Western Europe, socialism must advance on a broad front not only internally but also externally, perhaps on what is called the Mediterranean flank stretching from Portugal and Spain through France, Italy, and Greece."* The Romanian professor noted further that *"Italy may be the first crack in the Western world."*[91]

There were many cases of clear-cut cooperation between Moscow and Bucharest, despite noises of *"independence"* and the occasional strategic anti-Soviet pronouncement by Ceausescu. In 1980, British Labor MP Mark Hughes reported that British beef was exported to Romania, who then transshipped it to the Soviet Union.[92]

In April 1983, a well-placed Romanian in military circles admitted to former Ambassador Funderburk that Ceausescu was pro-Soviet; that Moscow controlled Romania through the Securitate; that Romanian spies in France transmitted information to the Soviet Union via Aeroflot; that all of the Romanian officials who studied in the USSR were placed in high-level positions; and that Ceausescu was *"very well viewed"* by the Soviets and was chosen to be Moscow's handpicked successor after the death of Gheorghiu Dej in 1965. It was reported that Ceausescu spent 2 years studying in the USSR and resided in Leningrad while collaborating with the KGB.[93]

Former Ambassador Funderburk also reported the depth and specifics of the continued coordination and influence of Moscow in Romania: *"There are large numbers of nonmilitary Soviet personnel in Romania, both at the Soviet embassy and in hundreds of industrial factories. This information was ignored as far as I can remember. High technology that the U.S. traded to Romania or that Romania acquired illegally from the U.S. and European countries was transferred to the Soviet Union when requested by The Soviets. In fact some of the technology*

[89] Funderburk, David M. Pinstripes and Reds (Selous Foundation Press, 1987) page 49.
[90] Codrescu, Andrei. The Hole in the Flag (William Morrow, 1991) page 72.
[91] Kalvoda, Josef. Czechoslovakia's Role in Soviet Strategy (University Press of America, Incorporated, 1978) pages 239-240.
[92] "Invaders in Kabul Eat EEC Beef, MP Says" Times (London) July 9, 1980 page 5.
[93] Funderburk, David M. Pinstripes and Reds (Selous Foundation Press, 1987) page 44.

was commissioned by the Soviets for Romania to obtain from the West (including the U.S.)...According to more than one Romanian official who spoke with me in the strictest confidence, the Soviets and Romanians got together several months before the Olympic Games and decided that it was in both of their best interests for Romania to go. In that way Romania could continue to project the image of being independent, bringing credits and assistance to Romania which the Soviets would not have to provide. At the same time, Romania's going was no threat to the viability of the Soviet empire or to the control of the Soviet communist party. Romania got a lot of credit for doing what was in fact in the best interests of Soviet and Romanian communist policy and Soviet/Romanian disinformation."[94]

In December 1989 Gorbachev and Ceausescu held a meeting concerning the relations between Romania and the USSR and the state of the international communist movement. Despite Moscow's efforts to ease Ceausescu out of power, the USSR nevertheless continued to provide outward praise and support for the hardliners in Romania. Such accolades were even recorded in the secret transcripts of Romanian Communist Party meetings with their Soviet comrades. Gorbachev noted to Ceausescu that "*Comrade Ceausescu, first and foremost I would like to congratulate you on behalf of the entire leadership of Soviet Union for the successful finalization of your Congress. I believe that you are satisfied with the results of your Congress. Within Romanian society, among the Romanian communists, as our comrades have told me, the reaction to the decisions of the Congress has been a positive one. From me as well as from the leadership of the Soviet Union, I would like to communicate, to you and to the entire Romanian party leadership, a friendly salute and good luck in bringing the decisions of the Congress to fruition.*"[95]

Despite the occasional *"angry"* exchanges and *"independence,"* Romania continued to engage in intelligence cooperation with the KGB. Many Romanian DIE officers at regional and central levels attended special courses taught by the KGB and GRU.[96]

The DIE Branesti Spy School was created in 1964 on the Soviet model. It resembled a university campus whose students lived exactly like Americans, Germans, Frenchmen, and other Western peoples. This school had Western style golf, tennis, swimming pool clubs, movie houses showing foreign films, and Western style cafeterias. The DIE trainees lived, spoke, and dressed like the Western peoples. The DIE reportedly had dozens of rifles, handguns, machine guns, and submachine guns from the US, Israel, Japan, Italy, France, Britain, and Belgium. The DIE also possessed US-made radar systems, infrared and light amplifying equipment for infantry, armored cars, and artillery, and US-made laser aiming devices for tanks.[97]

In December 1958, the Foreign Intelligence Directorate (DIE) dispatched Major Mihai Caraman, a Romanian and Soviet KGB intelligence officer, to Paris, to undertake a huge anti-NATO sabotage operation. Caraman provided the Soviets with NATO strategic plans. The

---

[94] "Statement of the Honorable David Funderburk, Former US Ambassador to Romania" Congressional Record June 26, 1985

[95] "Minutes of the Meeting between Nicolae Ceausescu and Mikhail Gorbachev, December 1989" Accessed From: http://chnm.gmu.edu/1989/items/show/692

[96] Rodica Eliza Gheorghe. The Romanian Intelligence Services During the Cold War Georgetown University Washington DC April 16, 2010 Accessed From: http://repository.library.georgetown.edu/bitstream/handle/10822/553496/gheorgheRodica.pdf?sequence=1

[97] Pacepa. Ion. Red Horizons (Regnery Washington DC 1990) pages 173-176.

Romanians penetrated NATO Headquarters, the Secret Documents Section of NATO's Translation Bureau, the World Bank, the headquarters of the Organization for Economic Cooperation and Development (OECD), and the French Ministry of Economy and Finance. Until 1964, all of the intelligence that Romania gathered in the West was transferred to the KGB. It was reported that *"after 1964, Caraman continued to supply Moscow with intelligence through a back channel, in spite of Romania's claims of independence. Between 1958 and 1969, DIE demonstrated acumen in exploiting France's position toward the United States to weaken the Western bloc, to Moscow's benefit."*[98]

In June 1975, the Third Secretary of the Romanian Embassy in Oslo Norway Virgil Tipanut defected and revealed that a Romanian spy ring was responsible for the theft of technology, including that of North Sea oil rigs. This network used Romanian diplomats and students in Norway, Britain, West Germany, France, Sweden, and Denmark. Romanian agents also sought information on the Concorde, NATO radar guidance systems, West German nuclear power projects, and laser technology, which would have been of great benefit to the Soviets.[99]

It was reported that Ceausescu's Romania developed an atomic bomb with the assistance of Pakistan and Canadian nuclear technology. The Canadian nuclear technology was also passed onto to the KGB.[100]

The Romanian intelligence service was taught by the Yugoslav and Hungarian services to extract hard currency from Romanian émigrés abroad and even enticed them to return to their home country. Ceausescu allegedly stated: *"we cannot nationalize the assets belonging to Romanian émigrés, we cannot take over their properties…but we should find ways to make them pay for that."* Smuggling techniques were taught to the Romanian intelligence by their intelligence comrades of the Soviet KGB, Cuban DGI, Bulgarian DS, Yugoslav UDBA, and the Hungarian AVH. The Romanian intelligence also took over various state-owned transportation companies such as ROMTRANS (international trucking), TAROM (airlines), and NAVLOMAR (merchant marine) by the early 1970s. Seventy percent of the Romanian foreign trade personnel abroad were intelligence officers, while 38 out of the 41 heads of Bucharest's foreign trade corporations were spies.[101]

The Romanians were also involved in training Western Communists and international terrorists in sabotage and espionage. Training centers in Romania trained members of Western communist parties in sabotage, guerrilla, and diversion techniques. Communist parties that were favored by Ceausescu included groups from Israel, Spain, and Greece. Romanian diplomatic pouches were used to transport money, false passports, and other IDs to Western communist parties.[102] The DIE maintained a sabotage training camp near Snagov that was frequented by

---

[98] Rodica Eliza Gheorghe. The Romanian Intelligence Services During the Cold War Georgetown University Washington DC April 16, 2010 Accessed From: http://repository.library.georgetown.edu/bitstream/handle/10822/553496/gheorgheRodica.pdf?sequence=1

[99] McDonald, Congressman Larry P. "Romania Spied on North Sea Oil" Congressional Record September 10, 1975 page 28517.

[100] Cameron, Stevie. "Ceausescu planned to use Candu data for bomb, author says" The Globe and Mail (Canada) May 2, 1990

[101] Pacepa, Ion Mihai and Ledeen, Michael. "Rumania Reaps Rewards of Hi Tech Thefts" Human Events March 16, 1985 page 12.

[102] Pacepa. Ion. Red Horizons (Regnery Washington DC 1990) pages 239-240.

members of the Spanish and Greek Communist Parties.[103] Romania also provided training to Spanish Communist Party cadres in sabotage, bomb manufacture, weaponry, and urban street fighting.[104]

Romania also engaged in a *"two-faced"* policy in relation to Israel. Ceausescu bolstered his *"independent"* image when he retained diplomatic ties with Israel. However, the true motivations for Romania's diplomatic relations with Israel were provided by Pacepa. He revealed that the Romanian Embassy was maintained in Israel after 1967 to serve as a *"Trojan Horse"* to spy on the Jewish state and pass the information to Ceausescu's allies in the Arab world and the PLO.[105]

After 1979, the Romanian USLA (special anti-terrorist squad of the Securitate) began training its troops in Beirut, under PLO auspices.[106] A former Romanian intelligence official reported that 10,000 Arab and Islamic *"students"* resided in Romania under Ceausescu. The Romanian official noted that *"a large number of Arabs were trained in some camps, let us say two or three training camps, run by the DSS-Department of State Security."* These *"students"* were from Libya, Iraq, Jordan, Egypt, Iran, and the Muslim Brotherhood.[107]

Turcu noted that Securitate special troops originally consisted of university graduates. In the 1980s, Elena Ceausescu then ordered that factory personnel and young men from orphanages fill the ranks of the special troops of the Securitate. Ceausescu and the PLO also had an agreement where Romanian territory would be used by the PLO for *"logistical support."* Romanian-PLO cooperation started in the late 1960s. Syrian, Libyan, Iraqi and Iranian military and special operations units were trained at a camp near Buzau, in the Carpathian foothills.[108] The Securitate gave a training camp to the PLO at Baneasa, north of Bucharest. They also supplied the PLO with hundreds of forged passports and electronic eavesdropping equipment.[109]

Pacepa outlined the process of how Romania and other European communist states were delegated various tasks by the USSR: *"In the early 1970s, the Kremlin established a 'socialist division of labor' for persuading the governments of Iraq and Libya to join the terrorist war against the US. KGB chairman Yuri Andropov (who would later become the leader of the Soviet Union), told me that either of those two countries could inflict more damage on the Americans than could the Red Brigades, the Baader-Meinhof group and all other terrorist organizations taken together. The governments of those Arab countries, Andropov explained, not only had*

---

[103] Pacepa, Ion Mihai. Programmed to Kill (Ivan R. Dee, 2007) page 108.

[104] Moss, Robert. "The Rocky Road to Democracy" National Review June 10, 1977 pages 663-667.

[105] Kempster, Norman. "Defector Tells How Israel was Betrayed" Sydney Morning Herald October 15, 1987 page 12

[106] Rodica Eliza Gheorghe. The Romanian Intelligence Services During the Cold War Georgetown University Washington DC April 16, 2010 Accessed From: http://repository.library.georgetown.edu/bitstream/handle/10822/553496/gheorgheRodica.pdf?sequence=1

[107] Rozenman, Eric. "Ceausescu and the Arabs" The Jerusalem Post March 7, 1990

[108] Morgan, Dan. "Romanian Army Rankled by Interference; Defector Cites Long-Standing Friction Between Military and State Security Forces" The Washington Post December 24, 1989 page A24.

[109] Ellis, Richard. "Iron Curtain camp days are over for terrorists-Dolni Brezany" Sunday Times, The (London, England) July 22, 1990

inexhaustible financial resources (read: oil), but they also had huge intelligence services that were being run by 'our razvedka advisers' and could extend their tentacles to every corner of the earth…Libya was Romania's main client in that socialist division of labor, because of Ceausescu's close association with Colonel Muammar Gaddafi. Moscow kept Iraq. Andropov told me that, if our Iraq and Libyan experiment proved successful, the same strategy would be extended to Syria."[110] Hence, Romania supplied weapons and traded with most of the radical Middle Eastern regimes, such as Syria, Iraq, Libya, and Iran.

Pacepa also recalled that Romanian had particularly close relations with the PLO: "*the Romanian espionage service (DIE) was responsible for providing the PLO with logistical support. Except for the arms, which were supplied by the KGB and the East German Stasi, everything else came from Bucharest. Even the PLO uniforms and the PLO stationery were manufactured in Romania free of charge, as a 'comradely help.' During those years, two Romanian cargo planes filled with goodies for the PLO landed in Beirut every week, and were unloaded by Arafat's men.*"[111]

Pacepa provided an amazing revelation which seemed to indicate that Ceausescu advised Yasir Arafat to engage in strategic deception operations that would bolster his image in the West as a *"moderate"* Palestinian leader of whom the West and Israel could negotiate with. Ceausescu also counseled Arafat and the PLO leadership to implement fake "*splits*" within the Palestinian terrorist movement which would in turn highlight Arafat as the "*voice of reason*" in the eyes of the West. Pacepa wrote that "*In March 1978, for instance, I secretly brought Arafat to Bucharest to involve him in a long-planned Soviet/Romanian disinformation plot. Its goal was to get the United States to establish diplomatic relations with him, by having him pretend to transform the terrorist PLO into a government-in-exile that was willing to renounce terrorism. Soviet president Leonid Brezhnev believed that newly elected US president Jimmy Carter would swallow the bait. Therefore, he told the Romanian dictator that conditions were ripe for introducing Arafat into the White House. Moscow gave Ceausescu the job because by 1978 my boss had become Washington's most favored tyrant. 'The only thing people in the West care about is our leaders,' the KGB chairman said, when he enrolled me in the effort of making Arafat popular in Washington. 'The more they come to love them, the better they will like us.' 'But we are a revolution,' Arafat exploded, after Ceausescu explained what the Kremlin wanted from him. 'We were born as a revolution, and we should remain an unfettered revolution.' Arafat expostulated that the Palestinians lacked the tradition, unity, and discipline to become a formal state. That statehood was only something for a future generation. That all governments, even Communist ones, were limited by laws and international agreements, and he was not willing to put any laws or other obstacles in the way of the Palestinian struggle to eradicate the state of Israel. My former boss was able to persuade Arafat into tricking President Carter only by resorting to dialectical materialism, for both were fanatical Stalinists who knew their Marxism by heart. Ceausescu sympathetically agreed that 'a war of terror is your only realistic weapon,' but he also told his guest that, if he would transform the PLO into a government-in-exile and would pretend to break with terrorism, the West would shower him with money and glory. 'But you have to keep on pretending, over and over,' my boss emphasized. Ceausescu pointed out that*

---

[110] Glazov, Jamie. "From Russia With Terror" Frontpagemag.com March 1, 2004 Accessed From: http://www.frontpagemag.com/Articles/Printable.aspx?GUID=D162656E-9C26-4FF4-BE93-3C64CCC1FFCD

[111] Ibid.

political influence, like dialectical materialism, was built upon the same basic tenet that quantitative accumulation generates qualitative transformation. Both work like cocaine, let's say. If you sniff it once or twice, it may not change your life. If you use it day after day, though, it will make you into an addict, a different man. That's the qualitative transformation. And in the shadow of your government-in-exile you can keep as many terrorist groups as you want, as long as they are not publicly connected with your name. "[112]

Ceausescu received much praise from the West for his public denunciation of the Soviet replacement of Czech *"reformist"* communist Alexander Dubcek with a more outwardly pro-Moscow leadership. Behind the scenes, Ceausescu cursed Dubcek for potentially allowing unrest to enter Czechoslovakia, thus threatening communist rule. Ceausescu remarked sharply to Pacepa that *"I'm not some idiot Dubcek, to tolerate chaos and provoke counterrevolution."*[113]

The Ceausescu regime also took a hard-line position in respect to the suppression of dissent in communist Poland. A December 1981 meeting of the Romanian Executive Bureau of the Romanian Communist Party discussed the extent and payment for assistance to communist Poland. Ceausescu noted that *"In all countries, including capitalist ones, where this unemployment and this problem exist, this thing leads to anarchy, and all the other (things). The man who does not work talks to people, walks about on the streets, hangs out at cafeterias. That is why (the Poles) have problems with the young people, and with all the others...They have not managed to organize time, and duly use it. But this is another problem, and we are not going to discuss it now."*[114] In October 1989, Ceausescu proposed that the Warsaw Pact *"jointly act in favor of preventing a serious situation in Poland, in favor of defending socialism and the Polish nation."*[115]

The Romanians also called for assistance to the Soviet puppet dictatorship in Afghanistan. A leader of the Islamic Front movement claimed that Romanian troops fought alongside other communist soldiers in Afghanistan.[116] Ceausescu noted in July 1989 that *"Afghanistan's problems have not been solved, the intervention in Afghanistan by the Americans and other reactionary forces is continuing. This land needs our support. Romania will work at Afghanistan's side in every way it can to help it defend its independence and revolutionary achievements. We are in favor of national reconciliation, but not the coming to power of a government that would eliminate all democratic achievements. We support the government of the Democratic Republic of Afghanistan, but we wish to stress that all of these activities and the solution of problems in different parts of the world must not lead to the elimination or weakening of the democratic, progressive forces and progressive regimes of these countries, but rather to their consolidation, to the strengthening of their independence and sovereignty, to the cessation of all steps to support counter-revolutionary forces hostile to the state, and every interference in the internal affairs of these countries. Let me state my opinion openly. The fact that the United*

---

[112] Ibid.

[113] Pacepa. Ion. Red Horizons (Regnery Washington DC 1990) page 216.

[114] Minutes of the Meeting of the Executive Bureau (Politburo) of the Central Committee of the Romanian Communist Party" December 17, 1981 Accessed From:
http://digitalarchive.wilsoncenter.org/document/112070

[115] "Romania's Ceausescu Proposes Warsaw Pact Intervention in Poland" The Associated Press October 3, 1989

[116] "10,000 Cuban Troops in Afghanistan, Rebels Say" Christian Science Monitor September 5, 1980 page 2.

States of America and other imperialist countries are currently demonstrating concern for the elimination of conflicts does not result from humanitarian considerations or from a desire to promote the independent development of these countries. This is a new way for them to achieve their goals: undermining the democratic achievements of these countries, their independence and their freedom.[117]

The Romanians also maintained close ties with Red China, sometimes to the economic advantage to the Soviet Union. It was also reported that *"In exchange for its mediating efforts, the Romanian government asked for supplies of energy resources, namely coal, which China readily provided at no cost. This barter proved advantageous to the Soviet Union, since it could cut down its coal exports to Romania, which in turn reinforced the image of independence, especially within the Council of Mutual Economic Assistance."*[118]

CIA Deputy Director Ray Cline pointed out that Romania exported oil to North Vietnam, Communist China, and Cuba. Deputy Secretary of Defense Cyrus Vance and Interior Secretary Steward Udall were concerned that Romania could copy and re-export the drilling equipment to other countries, such as China and the USSR.[119] Between 1965 and 1972, Romania exported military and economic aid to North Vietnam worth tens of billions of rubles.[120] North Vietnam was an ally of both China and the Soviet Union during the Vietnam War.

A declassified communist bloc document dated from June 1974 revealed that Romania strongly supported cooperation between the USSR and China and asserted that the *"split"* between Moscow and Beijing was *"temporary"* and capable of healing itself. The document specifically stated: *"Romania sees China's policy as an effective instrument in the fight against imperialism and hegemony. Standing on the foundation of the existence of the 14 socialist countries camp, Romania expresses the opinion that the existing differences should not interfere with the strengthening and expansion of relations between parties and countries. The controversy between China and the Soviet Union is a temporary phenomenon and should not affect the development of the relations of states within the socialist camp."* The document also noted that Romania imported Chinese-made weapons, such as Shanghai-4 naval vessels. The document also pointed out existing Romanian-Chinese cooperation in the production of tactical missiles and their fuel. The Romanians exported to China small arms and ammunition.[121]

A declassified communist bloc document dated from 1977 also highlighted the close military cooperation that existed between Bucharest and Beijing: *"Military cooperation occupies a unique position in SRR-PRC relations, as a subject of dynamization in this field in recent*

[117] Speech by the General Secretary of the Romanian Communist Party and President of the Socialist Republic of Romania, Comrade Nicolae Ceauşescu at the Meeting of the PCC of the Warsaw Treaty Member-States
Bucharest, 7-8 July 1989 Accessed From:
http://www.php.isn.ethz.ch/collections/colltopic.cfm?lng=en&id=19041&navinfo=14465
[118] Rodica Eliza Gheorghe. The Romanian Intelligence Services During the Cold War Georgetown University Washington DC April 16, 2010 Accessed From:
http://repository.library.georgetown.edu/bitstream/handle/10822/553496/gheorgheRodica.pdf?sequence=1
[119] Ibid.
[120] Ibid.
[121] Intelligence Note, Polish Embassy Bucharest, "'Concerning Romanian-Sino Relations'" June 5, 1974 Accessed From: http://digitalarchive.wilsoncenter.org/document/116928

months, especially in connection with a 4-year agreement on cooperation. Last April, a mixed commission on cooperation and collaboration in the area of defense industry was established. Deputy Defense Minister for Arms and Technology, Colonel-General V. Ionel. Chairs the Romanian party on this commission. The intensity of contacts may be illustrated by the exchange of seven military delegations in 1977. Noteworthy is the fact that 52 Romanian engineers and technicians have been staying on the training course, organized by the Chinese defense industry, since July this year. The same number of Chinese experts is in SRR. This, of course, has probably an influence on the overall bilateral relations."[122]

Towards the end of Ceausescu's rule, the Sino-Romanian military ties were maintained. In mid-September 1989, Romanian Defense Minister Milea met with General Guo Linxiang, the Deputy Director of the General Political Department of the Chinese PLA. A Chinese report of the meeting noted that *"the two sides highly appraised the relations of friendship and cooperation between the two armies, two parties and two peoples. They pledged continued efforts for further development of these relations."*[123]

In November 1989, Ceausescu urged the Chinese communists to forge an even closer relationship with Romania. He stated that *"Right now, there are a lot of problems existing in the world. The international situation is very complicated. At this time more than ever we need to strengthen cooperation between Communist Parties and socialist nations."*[124]

Intelligence ties and technology transfer collaboration also existed between the Chinese and Romanian intelligence services. Chinese intelligence during the reign of Hua Guo-feng passed on samples of film acquired from Kodak to Romania. This film was sold to tourists and exported to acquire American dollars for Romania.[125]

In July 1989, Ceausescu also praised the healing of the outward Sino-Soviet *"differences"* on the grounds of support for the solidarity of the international communist camp: *"We welcome the development of relations between the Soviet Union and the PRC, between the CPSU and the Communist Party of China. We consider this to be a very important event, and Romania has, as you know, has always insisted that this had to happen. We welcome this course."*[126]

---

[122] Intelligence Note, Polish Embassy in Bucharest, "'The Current Status of Romania-PRC Relations'" December 23, 1977 Accessed From:
http://digitalarchive.wilsoncenter.org/document/116933
[123] "Chinese Army Group Ends Visit to Romania" The Xinhua General Overseas News Service September 15, 1989
[124] Lubman, Sarah. "Romanian president seeks China's help" United Press International November 18, 1989
[125] Pacepa. Ion. Red Horizons (Regnery Washington DC 1990) page 372.
[126] Speech by the General Secretary of the Romanian Communist Party and President of the Socialist Republic of Romania, Comrade Nicolae Ceauşescu at the Meeting of the PCC of the Warsaw Treaty Member-States
Bucharest, 7-8 July 1989 Accessed From:
http://www.php.isn.ethz.ch/collections/colltopic.cfm?lng=en&id=19041&navinfo=14465

Yugoslavia

In 1948, Marshal Josip Broz Tito, the communist dictator of Yugoslavia, and Joseph Stalin experienced a sharp break in their formerly close relationship. Both rulers were loyal communists and devoted to international revolution. However, Stalin desired total obedience from his allies in Europe and Asia and Tito refused to follow the USSR in every policy dictate. In the years following up to the split of 1948, Tito's Yugoslavia was closely aligned with the Soviet Union in every respect. Such an alliance stretched back into the closing years of World War II. In September 1944, Tito flew to Moscow in a US-made Soviet Air Force Dakota transport plane. Tito and Stalin agreed for a *"temporary entry of Soviet troops into Yugoslav territory."*[127] The Soviet troops that were stationed in Yugoslavia engaged in exploitative behavior, while Moscow's advisers initially controlled the workings of the Tito dictatorship. Burtakov was the Soviet adviser to the Department for People's Protection (OZNA) and was notorious for raiding Yugoslav mansions of jewelry, crystal, china, and rugs. The Soviet Ministry of State Security (MGB) had residencies in Belgrade, Zagreb, Skopje, and Ljubljana.[128] As of early 1948, it appeared that Moscow had solid control over yet another European nation in the wake of the Axis defeat in World War II.

Despite the split, Tito and his comrades remained loyal to the cause of global communism and did not blindly follow the lead of the NATO and the United States. Despite the Soviet-Yugoslav split of 1948, former Russian Prime Minister Alexander Kerensky perceptively remarked in 1952 that there was *"absolutely no difference"* between Stalin and Tito. Kerensky stated that the Yugoslav dictator used *"the same policy of repression, the same lack of freedom, the same political arrests as Stalin."* He also charged Tito as having the same revolutionary expansionist aims as the Soviets. Kerensky himself also charged that Tito's and Stalin's call for peaceful coexistence between capitalist and communist states was *"a trick."*[129] Even elements of the American political leadership expressed some doubts on the authenticity of Tito's conversion to a *"new"* type of communism and Yugoslavia's alleged *"tilt"* towards the West. Even after the Soviet-Yugoslav split of 1948, Ambassador Cannon referred to Yugoslavia's anti-American position on foreign policy as *"straight Kremlinity."* In March 1950, Ambassador Allen in Yugoslavia reported that the Yugoslav officials *"pride themselves on being strict communists and do not wish to be too chummy with the 'reactionary capitalists of the West.'"* He noted further that *"Tito and his clique, who are all old school commies, and still believe explicitly in Karl Marx and all his teachings are deeply suspicious of us."*[130]

Despite American and Western aid and technology transfers, the Yugoslav Communists espoused rhetoric and even implemented policies that were still at odds with the Western ideologies of limited government and free enterprise. The Yugoslav leaders and their controlled press also emitted *"anti-imperialist"* rhetoric that condemned the United States and NATO as much as the Soviet Union. In 1948, Tito spoke before the Academy of Sciences in Serbia: *"The revolutionary period in Yugoslavia has not yet been concluded. It will last as long as exploiting capitalist elements will continue to offer resistance and hamper the building of socialism in our*

---

[127] Gilbert, Martin. The Second World War: A Complete History (Macmillan, 2004) page 596.

[128] Andrew, Christopher. The Sword and the Shield (Basic Books, 2000) page 356.

[129] Weaver, Warren. "Tito, Stalin Alike, Kerensky Asserts" New York Times July 30, 1952 page 3.

[130] Brands, H.W. The Specter of Neutralism (Columbia University Press, 1989) pages 165-166.

country. It will last as long as such capitalist elements are not completely defeated."[131] The Yugoslav Communist Party encouraged contacts with *"all the progressive democratic movements in the world."* At the Third Plenum of the KPJ CC in December 1949, Kardelj observed a *"tendency among the imperialists to exploit the contradictions between the socialist states, very much in the same way as we wish to exploit the internal contradictions of the imperialist system."* Tito warned that the Communist Party of Yugoslavia needed to be *"on guard especially among the younger members of the party that we do not forget that we are a socialist country in view of our new stand toward the imperialist world."*[132]

Tito stated in September 1951 that: *"When we speak about the democratization of our country that question should be rightly understood. We may have been too hasty in the application of some of our dictatorial methods,* **_but there is no question for us of turning toward a form of Western democracy. We are a socialist country, building socialism and ultimately striving to attain the higher goal of socialism, which is Communism_**.*"*[133]

In 1951, Tito stated that *"...Reactionary propaganda started to take root here and there; but we shall slowly have to cut those roots out because they were often ill intentioned...The radio of Western countries speaks favorably about us chiefly when we quarrel with the Russians...but when it is a question of our actual way of life or about our Socialist construction then there is very little which is favorable."*[134]

In 1954, Tito declared to the Central Committee of the Communist League that: *"From the West they want us to establish a multiparty system and even alone without us, that is in their fantasy they are creating here some illegal parties and multiparty systems."* Tito called for the acceleration of communism in Yugoslav institutions in order to triumph over remaining *"rotten anarcho-democratic and petit bourgeois"* ideas.[135]

In 1953, Tito stated at the Fourth Congress of the People's Front *"I consider today's international situation to be so alarming not only where peace is directly concerned but even for further progressive development in general as to make the cooperation of all progressive forces in the world indispensable."* Tito lambasted the *"most reactionary circles...with the Vatican at their head"* for opposing the world progressive movements and Yugoslav Communism.[136]

Even in the early 1950s, the Yugoslav communists launched anti-American and anti-Western internal actions that were directed at oppositional ideas, personalities, and culture. In 1951, sixteen former Royal Yugoslav Army officers were tried by the communists on the charge that they were plotting with the United States and France to overthrow the Tito regime.[137] In 1953, the Tito government launched an anti-Western and anti-US campaign against *"trashy"* and

---

[131] Handler, M.S. "Tito Warns Foes on Right and Left" New York Times November 12, 1948 page 7.

[132] Banac, Ivo. With Stalin Against Tito: Cominformist Splits in Yugoslav Communism (Cornell University Press, 1988) pages 137-139.

[133] Raditsa, Bogdan. "What Price Tito?" The American Mercury May 1952 page 37.

[134] "Marshal Tito and West Propaganda" The Times (London) October 9, 1951 page 5.

[135] Raymond, Jack. "Tito Links Plots to East and West" New York Times March 31, 1954 page 11.

[136] "Marshal Tito's Call" The Times (London) February 23, 1953 page 6.

[137] "Yugoslavs Try Royalists" New York Times January 26, 1951 page 4.

"foreign supported" literature and publications.[138] Milovan Djilas noted in 1952 that bourgeois democracy *"already belonged to the past."*[139]

Perhaps inexplicably, Tito and his comrades maintained an appearance of an outward loyalty to the USSR and its Eastern European satellites in the early years of the split. In November 1948, Foreign Minister Kardelj congratulated the USSR and wished that country every success in the fight of the *"progressive forces"* against the forces of *"aggression and war mongering."*[140] In March 1949, the Yugoslav government publically opposed NATO as a threat to peace and the Marshall Plan for Europe as interfering with the independence of its member countries. Yugoslavia also declared its loyalty to the East bloc stating: *"Yugoslavia is and remains an integral part of the Socialist bloc and could in no circumstances become a link between the two camps."*[141] Sometimes these pro-Soviet, anti-Western assertions translated into actual anti-American votes in the United Nations (UN) by the Yugoslav delegates. In June 1950, Ales Bebler, the Yugoslav UN Ambassador voted against the resolution that called for the use of armed force to repel the North Korean attack against the South. Another Yugoslav communist official lambasted the *"new imperialism,"* which he described as Western assistance for *"reactionary elements"* in the Far East.[142] Even stranger were the occasional reports of continued economic relations between Moscow and Belgrade, despite the split and the Soviet attempts to assassinate Tito. For example, the USSR shipped 200 tons of chrome steel to the Yugoslav firm Jugometal in August 1951.[143]

Tito and his propagandists also prided themselves on the creation of a form of an alternative, de-centralized communism called the Self-Management System. In actuality, the Self-Management System of Kardelj and Tito was also a sham, where the ultimate, central control remained with the Party bosses and state officials. Kardelj advocated scientific planning where compacts were drawn up according to the collective national plan. However, some Western observers saw through the charade of the alleged decentralization of the Self-Management System. Professor Harold Lydall noted that the Self-Management System was a *"vast public relations exercise."*

The industrial sector was organized into cartels where delegates from each branch of industry would dictate prices, distribution of hard currency, foreign trade, wages, and investment plans. Banks were organized into Financial Associations of Associated Labor. In the 1960s, the Yugoslavs strove to centralize industries into amalgamated giants. In the 1970s, industries were then broken up into Basic Organization of Associated Labor. According to sociology professor Neca Jovanov, these decentralized firms were controlled by an aktiv of the director and his aides; chairman of the workers council; and a secretary of the League of Yugoslav Communists.

---

[138] Raymond, Jack. "Belgrade Purges 'Trashy' Reading" New York Times July 6, 1953 page 9.

[139] "Yugoslavs to Spur Party on Ideology" New York Times August 25, 1952 page 5.

[140] Handler, M.S. "Tito Felicitates Russian Leaders" New York Times November 7, 1948 page 31.

[141] "Yugoslavs Voice Loyalty to East" New York Times March 23, 1949 page 20.

[142] Lees, Lorraine M. Keeping Tito Afloat: The United States, Yugoslavia, and the Cold War (Penn State Press, 2010) page 88.

[143] Radio Free Europe Research August 7, 1951 Chrome Steel Sold by Yugoslavia to USSR Accessed From: http://www.osaarchivum.org/greenfield/repository/osa:dabe0383-b55b-49a3-a538-3d4d9a54ec01

Even into the 1980s, the Yugoslav communists maintained their ingrained authoritarian tendencies. Three Yugoslav professors in 1983 were instructed by their embassy in London not to speak with *"class enemies"* During a Bradford University (Britain) conference titled <u>Open Socialism</u>. A young communist party official responded to Beloff's question in 1983 *"what right have the communists to monopolize power?"* with *"We won the revolution."*[144]

Even during the *"reforms"* of 1989 and 1990, the Yugoslav Communists remained loyal to Marxism-Leninism and the concept of the socialist economy. In December 1989, the 10th Macedonian League of Communists Congress, Pancevski noted that *"as far as social ownership is concerned...it is of vital importance that the LC[145] energetically counters existing confusions and deformed ideas which see this form of ownership as an artificial economic category with no real prospects, etc, in other words which see complete re-privatization as the only solution or prospect. It is, it seems, being forgotten that the socialization of property in general and even in present-day and most developed capitalism is an immanent economic law and that for socialism social ownership is one of its main foundations."*[146]

In December 1989, Yugoslav Communist Nijaz Durakovic noted that *"the orientation towards the market, pluralism of ownership forms and a mixed economy is not any kind of capitulation of the system, not any kind of a restoration of capitalism and old relations. This is a necessary and legal process, a necessary stage of development and a way towards a greater efficiency of social ownership. In the end...social ownership as the dominant form of property will not affirm itself through any kind of proclamations, constitutional, legal or political orientations, but only through a greater efficiency in competition with other forms of ownership and within the same conditions. It is precisely on this that the fate of socialism in this area and the world will depend."*[147]

In 1990, the Yugoslav Communist Party split into different factions, based in part on regional and sectarian ideologies. One sectarian organization called the New Communist Party retained its loyalty to hard-line Tito-Communism. In July 1990, the New Communist Party of Yugoslavia observed that *"the idea of socialism is alive and indestructible but in practice to date it has been essentially betrayed and turned against authentic communists. For this reason we must go back to the sources of Marxism and fight for a society in which no one would lack material and spiritual goods, and struggle for a single and united Yugoslavia..."*[148] Other Communists would very concerned that the Gorbachev-inspired *"changes"* in Eastern Europe would result in an unintentional counter-revolution. In August 1990, the New Communist Party of Yugoslavia General Secretary Dr Mileta Perovic noted in the Belgrade newspaper <u>Borba</u> that *"anti-communist counter-revolution is raging in Eastern European countries and could lead to a civil-war bloodbath not only in those countries but also beyond, unless checked."*[149]

By 1990, Serbian Communist Party boss Slobodan Milosevic became the ruler of what became the rump Yugoslav state based in Serbia and Montenegro. In the same year, the Yugoslav Communist Party became the Socialist Party of Serbia (SPS). The SPS and its leadership urged a continued loyalty to socialism and opposition to free market capitalism. In

---

[144] Beloff, Nora. <u>Tito's Flawed Legacy</u> (Westview Press, 1985) pages 229-237 and 24-26.
[145] LC was the acronym for the official League of Yugoslav Communists.
[146] "Speech by Milan Pancevski" <u>Tanjug</u> December 11, 1989
[147] "Opening Speech by Nijaz Durakovic" <u>Tanjug</u> December 13, 1989
[148] "Foundation of 'New Communist Movement'" <u>Yugoslav News Agency</u> July 7, 1990
[149] "New Communist Party of Yugoslavia legalized" <u>Yugoslav News Agency</u> August 3, 1990

November 1990, Serbian President and Socialist Party leader Slobodan Milosevic noted that *"Serbia could not afford to embark, via reforms, on ill-considered experiments in the spirit of some sort of primitive market liberalism, which has long been abandoned by developed capitalist countries. It (Serbia) will certainly not do this at the expense of getting the majority of employees and their families into a hopeless situation."*[150]

After the death of Stalin in 1953, the new Soviet rulers under Khrushchev, Malenkov, and Bulganin sought to mend fences with Tito. They were impressed by the Yugoslav dictator's success in implementing communism while receiving aid and weapons from the West and the United States. The Soviets quietly engaged in a rapprochement with Tito, while Yugoslavia continued to occasionally publicize assertions of a continued *"independence"* from Moscow. The post-1953 assertions of *"independence"* by the ruling communists in Belgrade were more than likely a deception by the Yugoslav and Soviet Communist Parties. This was confirmed by at least two communist defectors. Top Yugoslav defector Bogdan Raditsa noted in 1954 that he was privy to smuggled documents from contacts in the intelligence service (UDBA) and the Central Committee of the League of Yugoslav Communists. These documents laid out the specifics of a coordinated Soviet-Tito deception strategy laid down in the wake of Stalin's death. Tito and Malenkov were said to have agreed on resumption of the old Soviet-Yugoslav ties and all future, *bona fide* disagreements were to be resolved by a joint commission. This new found collaboration was to be covered up from the international arena. Furthermore, Tito was allowed to make occasional criticisms of the Soviets as a means of ensuring plausible denial of the new Moscow-Belgrade alliance. Hence, the West and the United States would continue aid to Yugoslavia. Tito would continue to assist the Soviets by disrupting NATO and cooperating with non-communist radicals in Europe and Asia to bring about an eventual socialist revolution. Malenkov also appreciated Tito's achievement of influencing Asian socialists towards the positions of neutralism and anti-Americanism.[151]

KGB planner Golitsyn also seemed to confirm the tenor of Raditsa's revelations. Former KGB Major Anatoli Golitsyn noted: *"It is clear from Yugoslavia's actions in the following months that she had in fact realigned herself with the communist bloc, including China. In September 1957 there were four strong indications of this: a Yugoslav delegation led by Vukmanovic-Tempo was welcomed in Peking; Yugoslavia blocked a United Nations resolution condemning Soviet intervention in Hungary; Yugoslav representatives attended a session of Comecon; and Tito, together with Gomulka, publicly repudiated 'national communism.' Said Tito, 'We think it wrong to isolate ourselves from the great possibilities of strengthening socialist forces throughout the world.' In October the Yugoslavs honored the commitment they had made to the Soviets in 1955-56 to recognize East Germany. In June 1958 Tito tacitly assented to the execution of the former Hungarian premier, Imre Nagy, whom the Yugoslavs had earlier betrayed to the Soviets."*

Golitsyn also noted that *"Yugoslavia signed the Peace Manifesto of the sixty-four communist parties, but not the declaration of the bloc communist parties. The absence of Yugoslavia's signature from the bloc declaration contributed to Western acceptance of the subsequent Soviet-Yugoslav dispute as genuine. However, in his lecture at the KGB Institute in December 1957, General Kurenkov made it clear that the Yugoslavs fully agreed with the*

---

[150] "Slobodan Milosevic on Yugoslav Federation" <u>Tanjug</u> November 3, 1990
[151] Raditsa, Bogdan. "Tito's Secret Alliance with Moscow: The Inside Story" <u>The Freeman</u> January 11, 1954 pages 263-264.

declaration but had abstained from signing it because they had reached a secret understanding with the Soviets that it would be tactically advantageous for them not to sign...From conversations in 1959 with Colonel Grigorenko, the deputy head of the KGB's disinformation department, the author learned that there were consultations and agreements between the Soviets and Yugoslavs in late 1957 and early 1958 on political cooperation between them within the framework of the long-range policy. The agreements covered cooperation in three fields: in diplomacy, particularly with regard to Egypt and India, and Arab and Asian countries generally; in dealings with Western socialists and trade unionists; and in the field of disinformation. According to Grigorenko, early in 1958 the Presidium of the CPSU's Central Committee had given instructions to Pushkin, the head of the party's newly created Department of Active Operations, to prepare disinformation operations on Soviet-Yugoslav relations in accordance with the requirements of bloc policy. This instruction preceded the outbreak of the dispute in April 1958."[152] It is significant that aspects of Golitsyn's revelations in respect to the real motivations for Yugoslav cooperation with the Third World and Western socialists and trade unionists dovetailed with that of Bogdan Raditsa's testimony.

Tito clearly aligned himself with the interests of international communism led by the great powers of the Soviet Union and Red China. KGB defector Major Anatoli Golitsyn noted that *"For the duration of the genuine Tito-Stalin split, it would have been more than Tito's life was worth for him to have attempted to visit the Soviet Union; but since 1961, Tito, until his death, and other Yugoslav leaders have been almost annual visitors. Khrushchev, Brezhnev, Kosygin, and Gromyko in their turn have been to Yugoslavia. Tito and his subordinates have traveled often to other communist countries, including, from 1970 on, China. Tito's death did not destroy the pattern; in April 1982 Gromyko visited Yugoslavia and the Yugoslav defense minister visited Moscow despite alleged differences over Afghanistan and Poland."*[153]

Golitsyn also noted: *"On important issues, Tito's line was consistently anti-Western and helpful to the fulfillment of long-range communist policy. He took up an anti-American position in the Cuban crisis of 1962. He followed the pro-Arab communist line in 1967 and broke off diplomatic relations with Israel. He worked hard to persuade the nonaligned nations to follow suit. In 1973 eighteen African states broke off relations with Israel. Tito followed the communist line on the recognition of East Germany and influenced many Arab and African states in the same direction. He mobilized the non-aligned nations in condemning American intervention in Vietnam. He criticized American behavior over the civil war in Angola in 1975, and for a while the Ford Administration reconsidered its attempts to improve relations with Yugoslavia."*

Formerly secret documents also pointed to Yugoslav-Soviet agreement in the area of the imposition of global communism. In 1956, Khrushchev noted in a meeting with Tito: *"...A camp of capitalism exists. And between us are the countries which can arbitrarily be called transitional, on which the socialist camp should exert its influence. This is the alignment of forces. All the socialist countries (here I listed almost all the countries of the people's democracies except Yugoslavia) should unite toward a common goal in the struggle against imperialism and for the victory of Communism."* Tito then declared: *"And including us."*[154] In a

---

[152] Golitsyn, Anatoli. <u>New Lies for Old</u> (Clarion House: Atlanta GA 1984) Accessed From: www.spiritoftruth.org/newlies4old.pdf

[153] Ibid.

[154] "Note from N. Khrushchev to the CPSU CC Presidium regarding conversations with Yugoslav leaders in the Crimea" October 8, 1956 Accessed From:

meeting with Tito, Khrushchev also asserted that *"On many questions of foreign policy we speak a common language."*[155]

In a meeting with Tito, Romanian communist dictator Nicolae Ceausescu admitted that the Romanian intelligence service's (DIE) mission was *"to build communism with capitalism's political help, money, and technology through influence operations."* Tito noted that ***"We wouldn't be able to get anything from the West by riding on Moscow's coattails and without Western money and technology there wouldn't be any communist society in our countries. That's why we should have our own way of dealing with capitalism."*** Ceausescu then responded *"Letting the West believe that we're different, that we don't want its scalp."* Tito then elaborated with his outline on the strategy of duping the West and the United States to the long range benefit of communism: ***"They call it 'Tito's Triangle.' I set up three basic guidelines: friendly smile toward the West, maximum take from it, and no contamination from capitalism…But that's not something we want to talk about out loud-not here on this yacht and not even in our deepest sleep. Let our men work together. They know what we need and they can keep their mouths shut.***"[156]

Yugoslavia also asserted its desire to cooperate with the rest of the communist bloc to impose international Red rule in the West and the United States. Before leaving for a visit with the Soviet communist leadership in Moscow, Yugoslav Foreign Minister Koca Popovic noted that this trip *"would afford the leaders of the two countries many opportunities to discuss the possibilities for the achievement of Socialism in the world."* Tito noted in Leningrad that *"we will do everything and strive to make the friendship between our peoples become closer, to make our cooperation useful for both sides and for the construction of Socialism and Communism."*[157]

Pravda noted on February 10, 1963 that *"Yugoslavia's stand on the main international problems, war and peace, peaceful coexistence, disarmament, abolition of colonialism, the German problem and number of other questions is identical with or close to the positions of the USSR and the other socialist countries. The Yugoslav leaders are taking steps to strengthen economic, cultural and political contacts with the countries of socialism."*[158]

In April 1974, the Soviet Army newspaper Red Star printed an article by Colonels Leontyev and Ponomarev reviewed Yugoslav-Italian territorial disagreements. The Soviets supported the Yugoslav position *vis a vis* Italy. The Colonels noted that the dispute *"again confirms the vital need to consolidate the principles on relations of peaceful cooperation for all European countries which is persistently supported by the Soviet Union and other countries of the socialist community…Of foremost importance are such principles as sovereign equality,*

---

http://legacy.wilsoncenter.org/va2/index.cfm?topic_id=1409&fuseaction=home.document&identifier=E5014604-F955-6B0D-FEB2186502C5537D&sort=collection&item=Nikita%20Khrushchev%20Collection

[155] Golitsyn, Anatoli. New Lies for Old (Clarion House: Atlanta GA 1984) Accessed From http://www.spiritoftruth.org/newlies4old.pdf

[156] Pacepa. Ion. Red Horizons (Regnery Washington DC 1990) pages 349-350.

[157] Fotitch, Constantin. "The Truth About Tito" The American Mercury February 1957 pages 93-98.

[158] Sleeper, Raymond. A Lexicon of Marxist-Leninist Semantics (Western Goals 1983) page 348.

rejections of use of threat of force, and finally, the basic principle for maintaining peace and security in Europe-the inviolability of borders."[159]

A Yugoslav Communist Party theoretician Dr. Ranko Petrovic noted in the article titled *"From Karlovy Vary to Moscow"* that *"only a dialectical analysis"* can explain why *"the position of non-alignment"* actually meant *"constant alignment in the struggle for peace and progress."* He also noted that *"In this respect the Soviet Union and the socialist countries were in a position to be the most effective counterbalance to the aggressors, considering the involvement of the USA. Signing of the Moscow statement and attendance at the meeting in Budapest therefore comprised one of the most important aspects of mobilizing progressive forces against the perpetrators and instigators of aggression."* Yugoslav Communist Politburo member Nijaz Dizdarevic noted in NIN in August 1967 that *"it is necessary to adapt the nonaligned policy to the new situation in the world"* in order *"to fight imperialist aggression."* He stated further that *"one should find a way to fight every form of diktat based on the fact someone is small and someone is big."* He also welcomed De Gaulle's fighting *"American hegemony"* in NATO.[160] In other words, *"non-alignment"* meant the domination of the world by anti-capitalist and communist forces. It was not a true, honest neutralism as commonly understood in the West.

During conversations between Tito and Brezhnev, the CPSU boss indicated that the Soviets did not want to interfere with Yugoslavia's position in the Non-Aligned Movement (NAM). Instead, Brezhnev wanted the USSR to cooperate with Tito in harnessing the NAM as a tool against imperialism. Brezhnev indicated that the Belgrade meeting was useful for *"exchanging opinions on the means for further struggle for achieving détente i.e. Helsinki Accords..."* The Soviets expressed their desire to *"cooperate with Yugoslavia in the preparations for this meeting and to consult with comrade Tito...We should have coordinated action."* (Brezhnev noted the last point). Brezhnev requested from Tito *"a coordinated action plan."* The 1976-1977 Berlin communist and workers parties' conference, private meetings between Brezhnev and Tito, and bilateral consultations on the CSCE between the Yugoslav and Soviet foreign ministries all indicated that the USSR considered Yugoslavia part of the socialist community. At the same time, Tito tried to dispel that pro-Soviet image with his other benefactors in the Western countries.[161]

Even in the post-1953 period, some American officials and policymakers spoke out against Washington's appeasement of Tito and highlighted Yugoslavia's loyalty to anti-Western and anti-American causes. Former US Ambassador Laurence Silberman noted: *"Yugoslavia pursues a path calculated to injure...American interests. The two countries are at the same time tacit allies and active adversaries. They are allies against Soviet dominance of Eastern Europe, but Yugoslavs are almost invariably found on the opposite side of every issue in world politics that matters to the United States. Soviet efforts to bring their military force to bear outside*

---

[159] Radio Free Europe Research Communist Area April 17, 1974 Soviet Army Paper Supports Tito in his Dispute with Italy Accessed From:
http://www.osaarchivum.org/greenfield/repository/osa:2ed28759-4dc9-4cad-b6d2-50c7ba1e94fa
[160] Radio Free Europe Research Communist Area August 31, 1967 Yugoslavs Call for More Constructive Communist Aid to Third World and an Anti-Imperialist Front With Non-Aligned and Underdeveloped World Accessed From:
http://www.osaarchivum.org/greenfield/repository/osa:29a4d8f4-1f73-4a15-a09a-e8368472a6d4
[161] Vladimir Bilandzic, Dittmar Dahlmann, Milan Kosanovic. From Helsinki to Belgrade: The First CSCE Follow-up Meeting and the Crisis (V&R unipress GmbH, 2012) pages 93-95 and 79.

Europe have actually been aided by the Yugoslavs."[162] Belgrade continued to humiliate and embarrass the United States at international forums. Between 1981 and 1982, Yugoslavia voted with the United States only 4 times at the United Nations.[163] In 1983, Yugoslavia praised Cuba and Grenada and protested the American liberation of the latter nation from communism.[164]

Sometimes, even the American political class attempted to dissent from the Washington Consensus regarding Yugoslavia's alleged *"neutralism"* and *"non-alignment."* Such diversions received an angry feedback from the dictatorship in Belgrade. Yugoslav officials blasted the Republican Party platform in 1984 for listing that communist country as one of the *"captive nations."* The Yugoslav Foreign Ministry stated: *"Our public has received with surprise the mentioned stands...which neglect the basic facts well known to everybody and obvious truth about the history of the Socialist Federal Republic of Yugoslavia. Such an ignorance of the recent and past history of our peoples is amazing, and is neglecting the known role and activity of Yugoslavia as non-aligned and independent country, even more because this position of Yugoslavia is the basis on which successful development of Yugoslav-American relations is founded."*[165]

Even in the last days of the unified communist state of Yugoslavia, the USSR maintained a close relationship with the Belgrade regime. In late December 1989, Dusan Ckrebic, member of the Presidium of the League of Communists of Yugoslavia Central Committee visited the USSR and met with CPSU Politburo member Aleksandr Yakovlev. This meeting covered *"some general issues of the development of socialism in the modern phase as well; as the current processes of reform in socialist countries, especially in Yugoslavia and the Soviet Union...they had a friendly exchange of views on social changes in the USSR and Yugoslavia and on certain matters of Soviet-Yugoslav co-operation."*[166]

In November 1991, the New Communist Movement of Yugoslavia celebrated the 74th anniversary of the Bolshevik Revolution in the USSR. The Movement called upon *"progressive and humane people of the world to reject the onslaught of the dark forces of capitalism which under the slogan 'new world order' is creating fascism which is aimed at destroying the noble achievements of the Great October Socialist Revolution."* Diplomats from the embassies of the Soviet Union, Red China, Cuba, North Korea, Vietnam, and Mongolia were present at the celebration.[167]

After the Soviet-Yugoslav rapprochement of the mid-1950s, Moscow and Belgrade massively expanded their trade relationship. In January 1956, a trade agreement was signed between the USSR and Yugoslavia, in which Belgrade admitted Soviet advisers, technicians, and scientists, and farming experts. The trade agreement covered exchanges of goods, which cost $70 million. Yugoslavia was to deliver bauxite, cement, barite, lead, corn, beans, meat, tobacco, and cigarette paper to the USSR. The Soviets exported coking coal, anthracite, raw oil, artificial

---

[162] Bradsher, Henry S. "Yugoslavia Gives U.S.-Made Tanks to Leftist Ethiopia" The Sun October 5, 1977 page 23.

[163] Beloff, Nora. Tito's Flawed Legacy (Westview Press, 1985) pages 186-187.

[164] Ibid, pages 186-187.

[165] "Yugoslavia blasts Republican platform" United Press International August 29, 1984

[166] "LCY Presidium member visits USSR" Yugoslav News Agency January 9, 1990

[167] "New Communist Movement celebrates October Revolution - Soviet diplomats attend" Yugoslav News Agency November 11, 1991

fertilizer, tin, rolled iron, and manganese ore to Yugoslavia.[168] The trade relationship continued to expand well into the 1990s and early 2000s, which was the period when Yugoslavia was ruled by Milosevic and the SPS. In 1972, the USSR provided Yugoslavia with a credit worth $1.3 billion.[169] Yugoslavia became involved in COMECON in 1964 and trade with that economic bloc increased since that date. By 1983, COMECON countries were recipients of over 50% of Yugoslav exports.[170]

The Soviets and Yugoslavs immediately resumed joint military cooperation in the area of the transshipment of weapons to various leftist Third World dictatorships. Former Yugoslav press officer Bogdan Raditsa reported that *"the arms from Czechoslovakia to Egypt have been delivered from the Adriatic shores, the ports of Rieka, and Ploche...They have been delivered all the time. Everybody could see. Even the American observers who are in Yugoslavia know that these arms have been delivered not from Russia. Czechoslovakia has no ports and harbors to deliver. They go from Czechoslovakia to Hungary, down the Danube, right into Rieka. From Rieka they are shipped into Egypt. People who delivered them in Ploche and Rieka speak to the natives in Russian. They are not even Czechs. They speak in Russian."*[171] As of February 1956, the USSR shipped *"many"* MIG planes through Osijek Yugoslavia to Nasser's Egypt.[172] The Soviets were also granted basing rights at Yugoslav ports and airfields. It was reported that Tito opened up the submarine base Boka Kotorska up to the Soviets.[173]

Military cooperation between Belgrade and Moscow expanded in the 1960s right through to the early 1990s. In 1967, a Soviet military mission arrived in Belgrade, while three Soviet navy submarines visited the port of Herceg Novi.[174] Since 1974, Soviet warships and submarines docked and received repairs at Tivat Yugoslavia.[175] During and after the 1967 Six Day War, Tito attended two ministerial meetings of the Warsaw Pact. Tito reportedly pleaded for direct Pact intervention in the Six Day War as a means to assist the Arabs. Tito and the Warsaw Pact ministers blamed the Six Day War on *"a conspiracy of certain imperialist powers, the United States in the first place against the Arab countries."* The Soviet Air Force also commenced massive over flights through Yugoslav territory and used Belgrade's air bases for re-

[168] Radio Free Europe Research Russian Exports to Yugoslavia February 23, 1956 Accessed From: http://www.osaarchivum.org/greenfield/repository/osa:96911b62-c522-4911-b50a-8856a0e2cb8d

[169] Beloff, Nora. Tito's Flawed Legacy (Westview Press, 1985) page 176.

[170] Ibid, page 182.

[171] United States Senate, Committee on the Judiciary Scope of Soviet Activity in the United States June 12 and 14th 1956 GPO 1956 Accessed From: http://www.archive.org/stream/scopeofsovietact2730unit/scopeofsovietact2730unit_djvu.txt

[172] Radio Free Europe Research February 14, 1956 Airplanes From Soviet Union to Egypt via Yugoslavia Accessed From: http://www.osaarchivum.org/greenfield/repository/osa:42b05091-9943-43f8-a728-18a38aa23c94

[173] Testimony of Dr. Slobodan Draskovitch-House Committee on Foreign Affairs. "Mutual Security Aid Act of 1959" April 16, 17, 20 1959 (United States Government Printing Office Washington 1959) pages 1051-1055.

[174] Eder, Richard. "Soviet Military Men Visiting Yugoslavia" New York Times June 23, 1967 page 1.

[175] Browne, Malcolm W. "Yugoslav Dockyards Repair Soviet Ships" New York Times February 7, 1977 page 5.

fueling. The Egyptian Ambassador to Yugoslavia pleaded with Tito for no delays in these Soviet airlifts and Tito noted that *"as far as Egypt is concerned I am not non-aligned."* Yugoslavia declared further that *"Both parts of the planned and long range offensive strength of the imperialist forces in the world particularly the United States."*[176]

The Yugoslavs extended refueling and over flight rights to the Soviets in 1970 in order to resupply the Egyptian forces in the Suez Canal zone. During the Yom Kippur War of 1973, the Soviet flew over 1,000 planes over Yugoslavia to resupply Egypt and Syria.[177] The Soviets used Yugoslavia in the early 1970s for over flights of troops and weapons to South Yemen; Angola in 1975-1976; and Ethiopia in 1976-1978. Submarines and other Soviet ships docked in Yugoslav ports and the public was excluded from the surrounding areas.[178] Yugoslavia established a regular contract to maintain and repair Soviet submarines and submarine tenders in its shipyard at Kotor.[179]

In September 1976, Commander in Chief of the Soviet Navy Admiral Sergei Gorshkov visited Yugoslavia and inspected naval facilities on the Adriatic. He also visited with Defense Minister General Nikola Ljubicic and by Yugoslav Chief of Staff General Stane Potocar. In September 1974, the Chief of the Soviet Staff General Kulikov visited Yugoslavia and in 1975 commander of the Soviet airborne forces General Margelov visited Yugoslavia on the 30th Anniversary of Belgrade's liberation. Though officially denied, there were reports that disguised Soviet warships visited Yugoslav ports. In 1974-1976, Soviet submarines and submarine tenders were repaired at the Tivat Yard.[180]

In April 1982, CPSU Politburo member Nikolay Tikhonov met with Yugoslav Army General Nikola Ljubicic, who was also a member of the Presidium of the League of Yugoslav Communists Central Committee and the Yugoslav Federal Secretary for People's Defense. The Soviets and Yugoslavs *"exchanged views on matters of Soviet-Yugoslav co-operation, which is based on the principles of full equality and mutual respect and meets the basic interests of the Soviet and Yugoslav peoples. It was pointed out that in the conditions of the complicated international situation, the two countries' allegiance to the cause of peace and socialism is a firm basis for mutual co-operation for the purposes of preserving detente, curbing the arms race and ensuring international security."*[181]

In October 1982, a delegation of senior officers of the Yugoslav People's Army, led by Lt-Col-Gen Daljevic, Assistant Federal Secretary for National Defense, visited the USSR. The Yugoslav delegation met with Soviet Army General Yepishev, Head of the Main Political Directorate of the Soviet Army and Navy and Admiral Sorokin, First Deputy Head of the Main Political Directorate, and USSR First Deputy Minister of Defense Marshal Sokolov. The Soviets

---

[176] Beloff, Nora. <u>Tito's Flawed Legacy</u> (Westview Press, 1985) pages 173-178.

[177] Ibid, page 177.

[178] Ibid, page 177.

[179] "Yugoslavia: A Country Study" 1990 Accessed From:
http://memory.loc.gov/cgibin/query/r?frd/cstdy:@field(DOCID+yu0197)

[180] Antic, Zdenko Soviet Naval Commander Visits Yugoslavia Radio Free Europe Research September 6, 1976 Accessed From:
http://www.osaarchivum.org/greenfield/repository/osa:cc19479d-0525-45d0-aa07-d6c26525e50b

[181] "Yugoslav Defence Secretary's Visit to USSR" <u>BBC Summary of World Broadcasts</u> April 28, 1982

and Yugoslavs discussed the *"further development of friendly relations and co-operation between the armed forces of the two countries."*[182]

In February 1984, Soviet Marshal Sergey Akhromeyev visited Yugoslavia. He met with Admiral Branko Mamula, the Yugoslav Federal Secretary for National Defense regarding *"the world military-political situation, especially in Europe and the Mediterranean, and on further development of co-operation between the armed forces of Yugoslavia and the USSR. In the talks…the two sides noted the successful co-operation between the two armed forces and prospects for its expansion."*[183]

Even in the period of *"glasnost"* and *"perestroika,"* Yugoslav-Soviet military cooperation continued apace. In August 1986, Admiral Branko Mamula, Federal Secretary for National Defense met with Soviet Army General Aleksey Dmitriyevich Lizichev, Head of the Main Political Directorate of the Soviet Army and Navy.[184] In June 1986, the Chief of the General Staff of the Yugoslav Army Col-Gen Zorko Canadi visited the Soviet Union and met with Marshal Sergey Akhromeyev and other Soviet generals.[185] In November 1988, Soviet Army General Dmitriy Yazov visited Yugoslavia. The meeting participants outlined the *"current questions of co-operation between the armed forces of the USSR and Yugoslavia. It was stated among other things that relations and co-operation between the armed forces of the SFRY and the USSR were developing successfully in accordance with the good inter-state relations, and that all the conditions existed for their more substantial and comprehensive advancement. In this connection, the need and possibilities for establishing co-operation on a long-term basis, especially in the area of the military-industrial complex, were discussed."*[186]

In October 1989, Yugoslav Federal Secretary of Defense Col-Gen Veljko Kadijevic visited the Soviet Union and discussed *"issues of mutual interest."* Kadijevic met with Defense Minister Marshal Yazov and General Vladimir Arkhipov, the Deputy Defense Minister of the USSR. Tanjug reported that *"mutual satisfaction was expressed with the development of military co-operation between the Soviets and Yugoslav armies."*[187]

In October 1990, Yugoslav Defense Secretary, Veljko Kadijevic, met with Colonel-General Nikolay Shlyaga, Head of the Main Political Administration of the Soviet Army and Navy. According to the Yugoslav News Agency, *"Their talks focused on inter-army co-operation between the two countries. It was noted that the relations and co-operation between the Yugoslav and Soviet armed forces were developing successfully, in line with the two countries' good relations."*[188] In August 1991, the Croatian newspaper Vjesnik reported that *"numerous facts were pointing out that the Yugoslav Army was undertaking strategic preparations for a possible clash with the forces of NATO…the Yugoslav Army has during the*

[182] "Relations With Yugoslavia; Yugoslav assistant defence secretary's visit" BBC Summary of World Broadcasts October 23, 1982
[183] "Soviet Chief of Staff in Yugoslavia" Yugoslav News Agency August 9, 1985
[184] "Branko Mamula receives Soviet Army General Lizichev" Yugoslav News Agency August 11, 1986
[185] "Sokolov and Akhromeyev Receive Yugoslav CGS" Yugoslav News Agency June 11, 1986
[186] "Soviet Defence Minister's Visit to Yugoslavia" Yugoslav News Agency November 18, 1988
[187] "Yugoslav Defence Minister visits USSR" Tass October 18, 1989
[188] "Soviet military-political delegation in Yugoslavia" Yugoslav News Agency October 26, 1990

visit of Soviet President Mikhail Gorbachev obtained the most sophisticated MiG-29 fighter bombers, which have a range from Batajnica, near Belgrade, to NATO bases in Sicily."[189]

Moscow also directly supplied heavy weapons to the Yugoslav armed forces throughout the 1960s, 1970s, and 1980s. In the 1960s, the Soviets supplied Yugoslavia with T-34 and T-54/-55 tanks, modern antitank guided missiles, Osa Class missile boats, and MiG-21 fighters. In the 1970s, the Soviet Union sold the Yugoslavs Mi-4 and Mi-8 helicopters and SA-2 and SA-6 surface-to-air missiles. Since 1985, Yugoslavia received a license to produce a domestic version of the Soviet T-72 tank for its own use and for export. In the late 1980s, Yugoslavia received the new Soviet MiG-29 fighter. Polish, Czechoslovak, and Romanian weapons systems were acquired and incorporated into arms produced in Yugoslav factories. About 95% of Yugoslav weapons systems were imported from the USSR and Warsaw Pact countries. Between 1983 and 1987, the Soviets alone supplied Yugoslavia with 75% of its weapons.[190]

The Yugoslavs also engaged in military planning for potential invasions and occupations of foreign nations and sections of the noncommunist world. In October 1945, former Yugoslav Air Force Second Lt. Voyislav Ilitch defected to Britain and revealed that Tito planned to invade Greece. The Yugoslav Army Fifth, Twenty First, and Twenty Fifth Serbian and Lika *"Shock"* Divisions were shifted towards the Greek border in preparation for such an invasion. A Yugoslav bulletin board newspaper noted: *"The whole of Macedonia must be one unit. If necessary we will defend with our blood the rights of our brethren in Aegean Macedonia."* In order to strike Greek targets, Soviet-built aircraft were also moved to airfields in Mostar and Skopje.[191] In 1953, Tito declared that he would fire on Italian troops if they occupied Zone A of Trieste.[192]

In the early years of the Yugoslav communist state and even during the split (1948-1953), Tito and his comrades asserted that they would back the USSR and the Bloc countries in the event of World War III. In October 1945, Tito noted that the Yugoslav Army was *"an army which will be a worthy ally of the great and glorious Red Army."* In December 1948, Deputy Chief of Staff of the Yugoslav Army Peko Dapcevich noted that Yugoslavia was *"creating a socialist fortress in the Balkans and strengthening the communists in the world...(The Army) was preparing itself safeguard...the unhindered development of the USSR and Eastern European countries...together with the other socialist countries and all peace loving forces in the world."* General Slavko Rodich noted that the Yugoslav forces were *"a deeply revolutionary army...part of the armed forces of the socialist front."* Journalist John Gunther asked Yugoslav officials whether they would side with the United States or the USSR in World War III. He was told that the Yugoslavs would fight with the Soviets. Gunther was informed: *"Certainly...because we are real communists...Yugoslavia would prefer at present to fight on the Russian side rather than ours...because the Yugoslavs despite the Cominform quarrel, not only still of themselves as communists but as being better communists than the Russians."* In August 1949, Tito stated: *"Let it be known once and for all that we are standing in the camp of the progressive democratic*

[189]"Croatian newspaper claims JNA preparing for 'possible clash' with NATO" Yugoslav News Agency August 16, 1991

[190] "Yugoslavia: A Country Study" 1990 Accessed From: http://memory.loc.gov/cgibin/query/r?frd/cstdy:@field(DOCID+yu0195)

[191] Sulzberger, C.L. "Tito Said to Mass Army Near Greece" New York Times October 19, 1954 page 7.

[192] Raymond, Jack. "Tito Bars a Drive Into Trieste Now" New York Times October 19, 1953 page 5.

forces of the world and in the first place in the camp of the Socialist countries..."[193] Such sentiments even illustrated that in the midst of the Tito-Stalin hostility, the split between Yugoslavia and the USSR was subject to being healed under the rubric of international solidarity in the event of a war against capitalism.

After the Tito-Khrushchev reconciliation in the mid-1950s, Yugoslavia placed itself solidly on the Soviet side in the event of a conflict with NATO and the United States. Tito stated in 1956 during a speech in Stalingrad that *"Yugoslavia in time of war as in time of peace, marches shoulder to shoulder with the Soviet people toward the same goal-the victory of socialism."*[194]

In 1956, Marshal Zhukov stated in the presence of President Tito that: *"Soviet and Yugoslav military forces fought shoulder to shoulder against German fascism. Soviet and Yugoslav military forces are struggling to maintain peace, but should war be imposed on us we will struggle shoulder to shoulder for the benefit of mankind."*[195]

Former Polish Z-2 (Military Intelligence) agent Pawel Monat reported that Moscow expected Yugoslavia to open its territory to Soviet troops in transit to their Western enemies in southwest Europe in the event of World War III. They expected Tito's willing cooperation in this endeavor.[196] Yugoslavia continued to express its attachment to the Warsaw Pact alliance, even without Belgrade's formal membership. In the mid-1970s Tito asserted to a group of visiting Czech officers: *"We are not formally members of the Warsaw Pact. But if the cause of socialism, communism, of the working class, should be endangered we shall know where we stand. We hold our aims in common with the Soviet Union."*[197]

Belgrade also supported Moscow's interventions in Hungary (1956) and to some degree, in Czechoslovakia (1968). Tito accused the Hungarian anti-Soviet forces in 1956 of consisting of *"fascists, imperialists and reactionary forces"* who were *"against Socialism in general...if with their intervention they saved Socialism in Hungary, then it was necessary and all this will one day become positive."*[198] Tito openly supported the Soviet invasion of Hungary: *"Of course if it means saving socialism in Hungary then comrades we can say although we are against interference Soviet intervention was necessary."*[199]

In August 1968, Tito spoke in Prague against the dangers of West German *"revanchism"* and *"Western imperialism."* In his talks with Dubcek, Tito was convinced that the Communist Party of Czechoslovakia was determined to prevent *"any attempt by anti-socialist elements to hinder the normal development of democracy and the normal socialist development."* Tito's deputy Kardelj noted that *"During the so-called Czech crisis, a search for a really democratic and simultaneously socialist way out of the troubles was made impossible by the inundation of*

---

[193] Draskovich, Slobodan M. Tito, Moscow's Trojan Horse (Regnery Chicago 1957) pages 127-128.

[194] Testimony of Dr. Slobodan Draskovitch-House Committee on Foreign Affairs. "Mutual Security Aid Act of 1959" April 16, 17, 20 1959 (United States Government Printing Office Washington 1959) pages 1051-1055.

[195] Raymond, Jack. "Zhukov Sees Tito As Ally in War" New York Times June 21, 1956 page 1.

[196] Monat, Pawel. Spy in the US (Harper & Row, 1962) page 187.

[197] Beloff, Nora. Tito's Flawed Legacy (Westview Press, 1985) page 176.

[198] Fotitch, Constantin. "The Truth About Tito" The American Mercury February 1957 pages 93-98.

[199] Beloff, Nora. Tito's Flawed Legacy (Westview Press, 1985) page 166.

empiricist liberal phrases. This, of course, subsequently meant calling in a third power on to the scene.[200]

Belgrade continued to export arms and military personnel to Moscow's allies in the Third World. By the late 1970s, Yugoslavia also supplied weapons to Iraq and Libya in exchange for oil from these countries. Iraqi and Libyan Air Force cadets trained in Yugoslav academies. When Qaddafi closed the Gulf of Sirte, Yugoslavia provided the Libyan Navy with contact mines.[201] Ethiopia, Egypt, Iraq, Libya, Angola, and India forged close military ties with Yugoslavia. The Yugoslavs provided arms and training for the armed forces of the above mentioned countries.[202] In the mid-1970s, North Korea acquired Yugoslav-built midget submarines for Pyongyang's Maritime Department of the 448th Army Unit and the 137th Squadron.[203] According to a Hungarian document dated from February 1980, Korean Workers' Party Politburo member Kim Yeong-nam met with his Yugoslav comrades to discuss various issues. As recounted in the document, one of the issues discussed was: *"in the sphere of military relations, the DPRK is particularly interested in the various optical facilities, anti-tank missiles, and laser technology. Kim Yeong-nam asked (the Yugoslav side) for assistance and an exchange of delegations in these fields."*[204]

Perhaps one of the most egregious aspects of the Yugoslav-Soviet-American relationship was the diversion of US-made technology and even weapons to the Soviet KGB. At the end of the late 1950s, it was reported that Tito passed on prototypes of American-made weapons to the Soviet Union.[205] Six Yugoslav companies reportedly diverted American computer and electronics technology to the Soviet Union in the 1960s.[206] In 1977, Yugoslavia transferred US-made M-47 tanks to communist Ethiopia, which was initially provided to Belgrade by American military assistance programs in the 1950s and 1960s.[207] Between 1969 and 1972, the Yugoslavs transferred American-made electronic equipment with military value to the USSR.[208] In 1988, a US-made computer that could improve the targeting of nuclear missiles was sent to Yugoslavia and then diverted to the Soviet Union via East Berlin and Belgrade.[209] In February 1988, the US Commerce Department busted *"an elaborate scheme"* to transship a high-technology computer system with military applications through Yugoslavia to the Soviet Union.[210]

---

[200] Beloff, Nora. Tito's Flawed Legacy (Westview Press, 1985) page 174.

[201] Ibid, page 177.

[202] "Yugoslavia: A Country Study" 1990 Accessed From: http://memory.loc.gov/cgibin/query/r?frd/cstdy:@field(DOCID+yu0200)

[203] Bermudez, Joseph S. North Korean Special Forces (Naval Institute Press, 1998) page 105.

[204] "Hungarian Embassy in the DPRK, Report 11 March 1980. Subject Korean-Yugoslav Relations" March 11, 1980 Accessed From: http://digitalarchive.org/document/116012

[205] Testimony of Dr. Slobodan Draskovitch-House Committee on Foreign Affairs. "Mutual Security Aid Act of 1959" April 16, 17, 20 1959 (United States Government Printing Office Washington 1959) pages 1051-1055.

[206] "Yugoslavia Russia Link Studied" Delta Democrat Times November 28, 1976 page 8.

[207] "Yugoslavia May Get More US Arms Despite Tank Deal" Yuma Daily Sun October 5, 1977 page 21.

[208] Ibid.

[209] "Feds Investigating Computer Shipment to USSR" Herald Zeitung February 23, 1988 page 2.

[210] Hobart Mercury February 24, 1988

Even during the real Stalin-Tito split, Belgrade did provide some assistance to the pro-Soviet Greek communist rebels. In February 1949, Greek communist rebels reportedly still used Yugoslav territory as a base of combat operations.[211] In the summer of 1949, a group of Greek Communists crossed into Yugoslavia and were then placed in a sealed train to Czechoslovakia. One of the Greek Communists noted *"Since there was no regular traffic between the two countries we could only assume that our departure was the result of a secret bargain struck by the Cominformists and the Titoists while they were publically exchanging the vilest insults."*[212]

During the real Soviet-Yugoslav split, Belgrade also launched influence operations to carve out a niche within the international progressive leftist and communist movements. In 1951, reports surfaced that indicated that Yugoslav agents infiltrated Greece and attempted to divide the Greek Communist Party into a reformist left-wing party. These agents were active in Salonika, Piraeus, and Athens.[213] In 1951, it was reported that Yugoslavia developed relations with the leftist parties in Europe, such as the British Labor Party, the French Socialist Party, the West German SPD, and the Italian Socialist Party. Tito stated: *"We consider collaboration possible with all progressive parties in the world and especially with the Socialist parties on condition that this collaboration aids strengthening peace in general."*[214] In 1952, Tito stated at the Sixth Congress of the Yugoslav Communist Party his desire to cooperate with *"progressive movements"* and Socialists abroad. He felt that Western democracy was an inferior doctrine and that its ideological influence needed to be resisted.[215]

Yugoslav support for pro-Soviet terrorists commenced once again after the Tito-Khrushchev reconciliation of the mid-1950s. Tito also funneled weapons from his own arms plants to leftist rebels in northern Africa and Indonesia.[216] The Yugoslavs helped launch the Red Brigades as a means of destabilizing NATO member Italy. The Yugoslav intelligence service (UDBA) infiltrated student Marxist groups at the University of Trento in the mid-1960s, which then led to the Red Brigades being formed in 1970.[217] In March 1984, a conference on the Movements of National Liberation was organized by the Yugoslav Communist Youth Federation. This conference hosted representatives of the FMLN, PLO, SWAPO, ANC, and the Polisario Front.[218]

In the name of anti-Zionism and anti-imperialism, Belgrade even provided aid and sanctuary to some of the worst and violent Palestinian terrorists. The Libyan agents who bombed the airliner over Lockerbie, Scotland used Yugoslavia as a base while they planned the operation. Yugoslavia provided Palestinian terrorist groups with paramilitary training at its Rangers School

---

[211] "Rebels Seen Using Yugoslavia" New York Times February 19, 1949 page 7.

[212] Radio Free Europe Research Eastern Europe Interview with Two Ex-Communist Greeks Who Were Trained As Spies in the Satellites March 5, 1952 Accessed From: http://www.osaarchivum.org/greenfield/repository/osa:a5293643-ebe9-4744-a506-dfb903d393ab

[213] "Yugoslav Agents Active in Greece" The Age June 12, 1951 page 3.

[214] Handler, M.S. "Tito Says He Backs Third Force to Bar East West Strife" New York Times January 14, 1951 page 1.

[215] "Marshal Tito's Survey" The Times (London) November 4, 1952 page 6.

[216] Testimony of Dr. Slobodan Draskovitch-House Committee on Foreign Affairs. "Mutual Security Aid Act of 1959" April 16, 17, 20 1959 (United States Government Printing Office Washington 1959) pages 1051-1055.

[217] Pacepa. Ion. Red Horizons (Regnery Washington DC 1990) page 354.

[218] Beloff, Nora. Tito's Flawed Legacy (Westview Press, 1985) page 187.

near Belgrade. Abu Nidal's terrorist teams attacked the Rome and Vienna airports from their base in Yugoslavia.[219]

Yugoslavia was known to have harbored and trained terrorists and other so-called national liberation movement fighters. They sheltered the violent Palestine Liberation Front (PLF) terrorist Abu Abbas, Ilich Ramirez Sanchez (Carlos), along with members of the Red Brigades and the Baader-Meinhof Gang. The Yugoslav Army's Intelligence Security Education Center trained 800 foreign soldiers from 10 countries and four liberation movements between 1960 and 1986. These foreigners were trained to be helicopter pilots, commanders, and officers. The liberation movements assisted by Yugoslavia included Frelimo, MPLA, PAIGC, SWAPO, ZAPU, ZANU, ANC, PLO, Tanzanian and Angolan soldiers, and the Chilean Socialists. When some of these above-mentioned liberation movements seized power, Yugoslavia was able to influence these new governments to purchase weapons produced by Belgrade.[220]

In February 1985, Yugoslavia reiterated its support for the Pan-African Congress (PAC) and other so-called *"liberation movements"* in South Africa. In a meeting with a PAC delegation, Dusan Dragosavac, a member of the Presidency of the Central Committee of the League of Communists of Yugoslavia (LCY) remarked that Yugoslavia *"will do whatever it can to supply help to the national liberation movement in South Africa."*[221] In December 1985, the South African judiciary accused five PAC terrorists of receiving military training in Red China and Yugoslavia.[222] As of July 1987, South African police Captain Buchner noted that PAC terrorists were trained in Nigeria, Sudan, Libya, Yugoslavia, PLO zones in Lebanon, and Democratic Kampuchea (Khmer Rouge-ruled Communist Cambodia).[223]

Even during the split (1948-1953), Yugoslavia subverted the United States through the American communist movement and resident émigrés. In the 1950s, the Yugoslav Embassy in the United States maintained 30 employees and diplomats. The Yugoslav UN Mission in New York hosted 12 diplomats and staff members. The Yugoslavs also maintained consulates in New York, Chicago, San Francisco, and Pittsburgh. Certain newspapers of the Yugoslav émigré community were also controlled by the communists. They were Narodni Glasnik (People's Herald) and Slobodna Rec (Free Voice). In the early 1950s, hard-line communist Yugoslav officers such as Vladimir Popovic and Peko Dapcevic came to the United States as members of military missions. Slobodan Draskovich believed that Popovic *"contacted people who in this country are spreading communism."* Dapcevic *"was accompanied by some other people who, even with himself, have been under suspicion that he is Cominform. There are other people — three members of the delegation who were known for their pro-Cominform sympathies. I understand nothing was done to prevent them from inspecting whatever they wanted to see. I also know of some individual cases of people who were known to be staunch Communists, who came for some military or other training; who contacted here in America, Communists. It is the military delegations, the economic delegations, the students. All those people, even in the period*

---

[219] Ellis, Richard. "Iron Curtain camp days are over for terrorists-Dolni Brezany" Sunday Times, The (London, England) July 22, 1990

[220] Lucic, Ivo. "Bosnia and Herzegovina and Terrorism" National Security and the Future 2001 pages 114-115 Accessed From: http:// hrcak.srce.hr/file/28807

[221] "Yugoslavia Supports Struggle Against Racism, Says Officer" The Xinhua General Overseas News Service February 21, 1985

[222] "Sentence of five PAC members on terrorism charges" SAPA December 16, 1985

[223] "PAC trial: security police operations in Bophuthatswana" SAPA July 11, 1987

of, let's say, 1948 to 1953, when Tito was considered to be an ally of this country, and they were allegedly banned by Moscow. They would come to this country and contact people who were 100 percent for Moscow. If they were against Moscow, they wouldn't be associated in this country with people following the Daily Worker line."[224]

Yugoslavia also developed communist networks inside the United States, even after the split with Stalin in 1948. Yugoslav representatives participated in celebrations of organized pro-communist Slavic groups in the United States. The main center of Yugoslav subversive activities was the American-Yugoslav Home, of which Consul Miodrag Markovitch was a frequent visitor.[225]

Within West Germany, Yugoslav intelligence maintained agents at their mission in Bad-Godesberg-Mehlem; the military mission in West Berlin; and consulates and trade missions in Munich, Stuttgart, Frankfurt/Main, and Hamburg. Yugoslav intelligence bases in France were centered at the Embassy in Paris, consulate in Strasbourg, the commercial mission, and their office for the Organization for European Economic Cooperation in Paris. Yugoslav spies were active in their embassy in Rome and consulates and trade missions in Milan and Trieste. Agents gathered information on Western intelligence services and NATO's order of battle.[226]

Cooperation between the Soviet KGB and the Yugoslav UDBA also increased by the mid-1960s. In 1966, it was reported that UDBA head Rankovic and the UDBA had strong links with the KGB and satellite intelligence services.[227] After the mid-1950s, the UDBA collaborated with the KGB and East European intelligence services in activities, such as preventing East European citizens who vacationed in Yugoslavia from fleeing to the West. When UDBA chief Rankovic was caught bugging Tito's headquarters in 1966, Brezhnev reportedly interceded on his behalf.[228] Federal Secretary of the Interior and Yugoslav Communist Central Committee member Franjo Herljevic met in February 1977 with KGB Chairman and USSR Politburo member Yuri Andropov to *"exchange views"* and to *"further promotion of relations between the two countries."*[229] During meetings with Brezhnev and KGB Chairman Andropov, an agreement was negotiated between the KGB and UDBA for the exchange of intelligence information. In advance of the CSCE meeting in Belgrade, the Yugoslavs and Soviets agreed to send and host a KGB operative working group. The KGB also shared information with their Yugoslav counterparts on fascist Ustasha émigrés in Western Europe.[230] In December 1986, the KGB and the UDBA agreed to cooperate against terrorism. This cooperation was the result of a meeting between KGB Chairman Viktor Chebrikov and Yugoslav Interior Minister Dobroslav Culafic.

---

[224] United States Senate, Committee on the Judiciary Scope of Soviet Activity in the United States June 12 and 14th 1956 GPO 1956 Accessed From: http://www.archive.org/stream/scopeofsovietact2730unit/scopeofsovietact2730unit_djvu.txt

[225] "Yugoslav Agents Aid Red Cause Here" New York Times September 18, 1949 page 2.

226 USAREUR Intelligence Estimate-1961 January 1961 Accessed From: http://www.php.isn.ethz.ch/collections/colltopic.cfm?lng=en&id=18700&navinfo=14968

[227] Radio Free Europe Research Communist Area August 1, 1966 Yugoslav State Security Service Purged: Had Links to Moscow Accessed From: http://osaarchivum.org/files/holdings/300/8/3/text/76-4-159.shtml

[228] Borowiec, Andrew. Yugoslavia after Tito (Praeger, 1977) page 100.

[229] "KGB Head Andropov Talks With SFRY's Herljevic" Tanjug February 24, 1977

[230] Vladimir Bilandzic, Dittmar Dahlmann, Milan Kosanovic. From Helsinki to Belgrade: The First CSCE Follow-up Meeting and the Crisis (V&R unipress GmbH, 2012) pages 115-116.

The Soviets and Yugoslavs *"pledged to consult each other, exchange information in fields of interest for security of the two countries, Europe and the world, and cooperate in the fight against international crime, and especially terrorism."*[231] In February 1989, a Yugoslav and an Italian were arrested for acquiring NATO documents that were then passed to the Soviets.[232]

Even the Red Chinese were willing to overcome their revulsion to aspects of Tito's version of Marxism-Leninism in the interests of communist solidarity. On July 30, 1977 Foreign Minister Huang Hua gave a speech to an audience that consisted of Central Committee members, military officers, high diplomatic authorities, and foreign trade officials. He stated: ***"Tito's visit represents the flexibility that is needed in our strategy and is not any way a form of political bartering. Although minor differences exist between our two nations we still have a common goal. We do this to achieve our objectives*** *..."*[233]

In 1978, the Chinese intelligence agencies established a regional base in Europe in Belgrade under Wang Chenxi. In the early 1980s, head of the International Relations Department of the Chinese Communist Party Qiao Shi and Minister of Public Security Tao Siju travelled to Belgrade to strengthen Beijing's ties with the UDBA. They met with the Security Chief for Tito Stane Dolanc and forged a permanent relationship with the Chinese intelligence service. These relations remained strong due to the efforts of Colonel Slavko Milojevic, who was also the Yugoslav military attaché in Beijing. [234]

Trade between Red China and Yugoslavia totaled $14 million in 1970. Yugoslavia also supported Red China's admission to the United Nations in 1971. In late 1970, the Yugoslav Communists supported an increased role for Red China's participation in world affairs. In 1978, Chinese Communist Party leader Hua Kuo-feng traveled to Yugoslavia and signed an agreement for the establishment of a Sino-Yugoslavian committee for economic, scientific and technological cooperation. Belgrade also praised Red China's breed of *"reformists"* such as Deng Xiaoping as socialist modernizers. The state-controlled Yugoslav media praised Deng Xiaoping as *"a man engaged in a great task of reform"* and *"a genuine Marxist."* A Yugoslav expert on China noted *"Marxism is not a dogma, rather it is a scientific, critical world view...In China, Marxist ideas are forging ahead, making the most daring ideological breakthrough from what was considered untouchable areas of truth yesterday. Since they renounced dogmatic concepts in 1978, the Chinese Communists have been making especially speedy development of Marxist ideas in the domain of economic theory."*[235]

---

[231] "KGB and Yugoslavs Agree to Cooperate Against Terrorism" The Associated Press December 5, 1986

[232] "Italy Arrests 2 Linked To Anti-NATO Spying" The New York Times February 20, 1989 page A6.

[233] Huang Hua Behind the Scenes of Red China's Foreign Policy The Chan Wang Publication Service September 30, 1978 pages 12-19.

[234] "Chinese Agencies Lose a Friend" Intelligence Newsletter November 12, 1998

[235] Pi Ying-hsien. "PRC/Eastern European Relations and East Europe's Views on China's Economic Reforms" Journal of Social, Political, and Economic Studies Volume 12 1987 pages 157-183.

China

In 1960, the communist world was struck with a seemingly major setback called the Sino-Soviet split. In the eyes of many American policymakers and intelligence officials, this event presented both a unique opportunity to further the dissension within the socialist community, while others feared that the *"split"* was a grand deception. The Central Intelligence Agency was the main battleground in the silent intellectual war over the validity of the Sino-Soviet Deception. The skeptics of the validity of the *"split"* were defeated, which then led to the ultimate decision to forge relations with the People's Republic of China as a means of containing and limiting the ambitions of the USSR. Meanwhile, the anti-communist movement in America was divided as to how to react to the *"split"* and to present the news of renewed American relations with the People's Republic of China. Some decided to support the notion of utilizing a *"China Card"* that would be directed against the Soviet Union as an exercise in Metternich-style *Realpolitik*. Other anti-communists, loyal to Free China in Taiwan, believed that the *"split"* was nothing but a grand deception whose ultimate aim was the crippling of the Free World and capitalism. In light of the alliance of communist China and the Russian Federation and their strategic positioning within the American economy, analysts need to explore the background and validity of the Sino-Soviet split of the old *"Cold War"* days. Next, such analysts need to review the evidence as to whether a) Would China would remain a non-hostile state *vis a vis* the United States? b) If the Sino-Soviet *"split"* was *bona fide*, would the two great communist powers eventually heal their conflict and unite on the basis of communist and anti-American solidarity? c) Was the Sino-Soviet *"split"* a strategic deception from the start, as former CIA Counter-Intelligence Chief James Angleton and Soviet KGB defector Major Anatoli Golitsyn charged? Based on the evidence presented in this essay, one can come to either one of the following conclusions: despite the pretensions of strategic convergence with the United States, China was irrevocably committed to the destruction of the capitalist and imperialist U.S.A. and the Sino-Soviet *"dispute"* was either 1) a strategic deception or 2) a conflict that could be healed under the rubric of internationalist communist solidarity. Indeed, the open *"split"* was publicly healed as the 1980s progressed and became an unrealized threat to the NATO countries, the continental United States, and the non-communist Asian countries. Such an anti-American axis developed and morphed into what is presently called the Shanghai Cooperation Organization (SCO).

Despite the romanticism of pro-Maoist American leftists and communists, the Chinese Communist Party (CCP) maintained a close relationship with the Soviet Union since the 1920s. Soviet support for Mao's Red Army and the CCP were crucial for the communist victory over the Nationalists led by Chiang Kai-shek. Mao Tse-tung received Soviet funding since 1921. One Soviet payment receipt was for $300,000 and was signed and sealed by Mao himself.[236] In 1934, Kuomintang secret police disrupted radio communication between Moscow and the CCP. In 1936, the radio contact was restored and placed under Mao's personal control. The Soviets used a *"foreign company"* to purchase and deliver military aid to the Chinese Red Army, which consisted of 550-600 tons of weapons. The Soviets also supplied the CCP with $550,000, which

---

[236]Mosher, Steven W. "The Real Mao" <u>Washington Times</u> October 22, 2005 Accessed From: http://www.washingtontimes.com/news/2005/oct/22/20051022-100239-6825r/print/

was channeled through agents in Shanghai in 1936. In 1937, the Soviets sent $800,000 via the Comintern to the CCP.[237]

After World War II and the defeat of militarist-fascist Japan, the Soviets stepped up its military assistance to Mao's Red Army. British intelligence reported that Northern Korean railways were used to transport Chinese Red Army troops to Soviet-occupied Manchuria in 1946 and 1947. Northern Korea also served as a *"reliable rear area"* for the Chinese Communists to acquire supplies such as grain and rest and recreation. In May 1947, the Chinese PLA used northern Korea to billet soldiers. Meanwhile, Korean grain and minerals was exchanged for goods manufactured in territories occupied by the Chinese Communists. Most of the output from the large Hungnam explosives plant was shipped to communist-held areas of China, such as dynamite and blasting fuses.[238]

In the period from 1945 to 1949, the Chinese People's Liberation Army sought refuge in the Soviet-zones of Manchuria, Port Arthur, and Dairen. Mao's forces were trained and rearmed in these Soviet-occupied areas. The Soviets turned over 900 ex-Japanese planes, 700 tanks, 3,700 artillery guns, mortars, grenade launchers, 12,000 machine guns, vessels from the Sungari River flotilla, and thousands of rifles to Mao's Red Army. Other weapons also originated from Soviet-held northern Korea and Moscow's satellite, the Mongolian People's Republic. Soviet-made arms were also shipped, along with captured Nazi weapons to Mao's troops. These ex-Nazi weapons were captured by the Soviets, who in turn, removed the German markings. The Chinese Communist Party (CCP) pretended that these ex-Nazi weapons were American-made arms captured from the Kuomintang. The Soviets also transferred tens of thousands of Japanese POWs to fight alongside Mao's Red Army. The Japanese served as flight instructors and created the CCP air force. Some Japanese served as combat troops and medical care units. As early as 1946, Mao begged the USSR to accept food exports from their liberated zones as payment for aid to the CCP. By 1947, the CCP shipped one million tons of food per year to the Soviet Union.[239]

In late 1945 and early 1946, the Soviets supervised the movement of 400,000 Chinese communist troops and 20,000 party cadres into Manchuria. The Soviets also built munitions plants in Soviet-controlled sections of Manchuria. In May 1948, the Soviets sent 300 economic advisers to Mao's forces in Manchuria.[240] A Chinese Communist Party document was captured by Nationalist forces and was dated January 1946. It spelled out an agreement between the Chinese Communists and the Soviet High Command, where Moscow was to provide 5,000 troops in the war against Chiang Kai-shek and the Nationalists.[241]

After Mao took over China in October 1949, the Soviet Union greatly expanded their military and intelligence relationship with Beijing. Chinese Nationalist intelligence reports indicated that as of June 1950, 12,000 Soviet advisers and technicians were assigned to the

---

[237] Sheng, Michael M. Battling Western Imperialism (Princeton University Press, 1997) pages 28-29.
[238] Cumings, Bruce. Korea's Place in the Sun (W. W. Norton & Company 2005) page 240.
[239] Halliday, Jon and Chang, Jung. Mao: The Unknown Story (Knopf Doubleday Publishing Group 2011) pages 50-55.
[240] Douglas J. Macdonald. "Communist bloc expansion in the early Cold War: challenging realism, refuting revisionism" International Security Volume 20 Number 3 Winter 1995 Accessed From: http://www.ihrr.net/files/2006ss%20/Challenging-realism-Macdonald-1995.pdf
[241] Utley, Freda. The China Story (Regnery Chicago 1951) Accessed From: http://www.fredautley.com/pdffiles/book02.pdf

Chinese People's Liberation Army, 3,000 were stationed with the Chinese Communist Navy, 8,000 to the Chinese Communist Air Force, 1,650 to Ordnance, and 5,000 to "*the political sphere.*" An agreement between Red China and the Soviets stipulated that each company of the Chinese People's Liberation Army was to be assigned a Soviet "*political adviser.*" Based on British, American, and Nationalist Chinese intelligence sources, this agreement also called for the "*complete cooperation between all persons of both countries connected with security.*" A secret treaty provision revealed that the Soviets would "*help solve the economic difficulties of the Chinese*" by providing "*employment*" for "*unemployed Chinese laborers*" in the USSR. This actually translated into the provisioning of slave laborers to the Soviet GULAG camp system/ When the 26th and the 27th Chinese Communist Armies rebelled in South China in 1950, the rebellious soldiers were shipped out to Soviet GULAG slave labor camps. If World War III erupted in Europe, China also agreed to dispatch "*laborers and expeditionary forces*" to serve under the Soviet High Command. The Chinese combat troops were to total 100,000 and 1,000,000 laborers would also be provided by Beijing to the European theater of Soviet operations in the event of World War III. The USSR and China also agreed to "*the intensive development of an International Army Corps with soldiers of all Asiatic nations serving in the ranks.*" Moscow and Beijing also agreed to plan "*all future military operations under a joint Sino-Soviet staff.*" The Commander of the Joint Forces was to be nominated by the Soviet Union and the Deputy Commander to be nominated by China. A Far Eastern Cominform was to be located in Red China to promote communist revolution in Asia.[242] In March 1950, the Soviet Union sent an air division to Red China, while Moscow's pilots shot down Nationalist Air Force planes.[243]

KGB defector Major Anatoli Golitsyn personally witnessed Soviet activities in Red China during the 1940s: "*While serving in the section of the Committee of Information that was responsible for counterintelligence work in Soviet organizations in China, Korea, and Mongolia, the author (Golitsyn) learned of a Soviet decision, taken after secret negotiations with a high-level CPC delegation to Moscow in the autumn of 1946, to step up Soviet military aid to the CPC; the Soviet general staff, military intelligence, and the Ministry of Transport were all instructed to give priority to the Chinese Communist army. In addition to the Japanese arms captured by the Soviets in Manchuria, large quantities of Soviet arms and ammunition, including American weapons received by the Soviet Union from the United States during the war, were secretly shipped by train to China between 1946 and 1949. In a lecture to students of the High Intelligence School in Balashikha in 1949, General Roshchin, the head of Soviet intelligence and Soviet ambassador in China, claimed that Soviet assistance had enabled the Chinese Communist army to swing the military balance in its favor and to launch its final and successful offensive against the Nationalist army in 1947-48...A major Soviet intelligence effort went into obtaining military information on the Kuomintang army for the benefit of the CPC and into the subversion of the Nationalist administration and police. When the Soviet embassy followed the Nationalist government to Canton, it did so not, as is often supposed, to demonstrate Soviet allegiance to the Treaty of Friendship with the Nationalist government, but, according to Soviet intelligence*

---

[242] Utley, Freda. The China Story (Regnery Chicago 1951) Accessed From: http://www.fredautley.com/pdffiles/book02.pdf

[243] Douglas J. Macdonald. "Communist bloc expansion in the early Cold War: challenging realism, refuting revisionism" International Security Volume 20 Number 3 Winter 1995 Accessed From: http://www.ihrr.net/files/2006ss%20/Challenging-realism-Macdonald-1995.pdf

telegrams between China and Moscow, to facilitate contact with Soviet agents in the Nationalist administration."[244]

Stalin personally endorsed the concept of providing massive assistance to the Maoist Communist regime: *"We will of course give the new China all possible assistance. If socialism is victorious in China and our countries follow a single path, then the victory of socialism in the world will virtually be guaranteed. Nothing will threaten us. Therefore, we cannot withhold any effort or means in our support of the Chinese Communists."*[245]

The Soviets and Chinese also colluded in efforts to communize Asia and even the rest of the world. In January 1950, Taiwanese intelligence received information that Stalin and Mao collaborated on a master plan to Sovietize all of Asia. The Soviets would provide China with assistance to communize that country, along with aid to insurgents who fought non-communist governments in Asia. Mao proposed to the Soviet dictator that he should dispatch 50,000 agents to China that would military advice to the PLA and to supervise the establishment of relations with foreign communists and leftwing fellow travelers. The remainder of the advisers would assist Mao in grabbing existing American and British foreign trade markets in China.[246]

Even towards the *"end"* of Sino-Soviet cooperation, the available declassified documents point to continued intentions for cooperation in case of World War III with the United States. Mao noted to Khrushchev in a 1958 meeting that: *"In case of war we should definitely cooperate."*[247]

Mao and Khrushchev then conversed about future wartime collaboration:
*"**N.S. Khrushchev:** I said that, when the war begins, we would have to use the coast widely, including Vietnam.*
***Mao Zedong:** I already said that, in case of war, the Soviet Union will use any part of China, (and) Russian sailors will be able to act in any port of China.*
***N.S. Khrushchev**: I would not speak about Russian sailors. Joint efforts are needed if war breaks out. Perhaps Chinese sailors would act, perhaps joint efforts would be necessary. But we did not raise the question about any territory or our base there."*[248]

It was reported that in a 1959 meeting, Mao and Khrushchev reflected favorably that communism made significant gains in the world: *"Overall, the international situation is favorable for the socialist camp, underlined Mao Tse-Tung. He said: 'Comrade Khrushchev and the CC CPSU undertook good measures in relation to the United States of America.' The imperialists, Mao Tse-Tung added, have many weaknesses. They have serious internal contradictions. A rapid swell in the anti-imperialist liberation movement is occurring in Africa*

---

[244] Golitsyn, Anatoli. <u>New Lies for Old</u> (Clarion House: Atlanta GA 1984) Accessed From http://www.spiritoftruth.org/newlies4old.pdf

[245] Douglas J. Macdonald. "Communist bloc expansion in the early Cold War: challenging realism, refuting revisionism" <u>International Security</u> Volume 20 Number 3 Winter 1995 Accessed From: http://www.ihrr.net/files/2006ss%20/Challenging-realism-Macdonald-1995.pdf

[246] "Sovietized Asia Plan Laid to Stalin, Mao" <u>New York Times</u> January 9, 1950 page 3.

[247] "First conversation between N.S. Khrushchev and Mao Zedong" July 31, 1958 Accessed from Cold War International History Project Database http://www.wilsoncenter.org/index.cfm?topic_id=1409&fuseaction=va2.document&identifier=5034C198-96B6-175C-9AB8386F9E8C7DBD&sort=Collection&item=The%20Cold%20War%20in%20Asia

[248] Ibid.

and Latin America. As far as Asia is concerned, continued Mao Tse-Tung, here on the surface there is a certain decline (in the movement), explainable by the fact that in many countries of Asia the national bourgeoisie has already taken power. This has not taken place in Africa and Latin America. These two continents present for the USA, England, and France a source of trouble and tasks which are difficult to solve."[249]

Even hints of a *"split"* between the Soviets and Chinese were carefully balanced with a strong commitment to the ideological alliance between Mao and Khrushchev. Mao Tse Tung noted in <u>An Outline for a Speech on the International Situation</u> in December 1959 that ***"The basic interests of China and the Soviet Union have determined that after all these two great powers should unite. Where they don't unite, it is only a temporary phenomenon, only one finger in ten***. *Study the Soviet Union's merits and support all the Soviet Union's correct positions. There are two good things about the reactionaries' anti-Chinese (activities): one is that they have revealed the reactionaries, reducing their prestige among the people; the second is that they have stimulated the consciousness of the majority of the peoples in the world, who can then see that reactionary imperialism, nationalism, and revisionism are enemies, swindlers, and contraband, whereas the Chinese flag is bright red.*"[250]

Even after the *"split"* commenced in 1960, the USSR and Red China continued to issue mutual, public statements which upheld their continued solidarity under the rubric of anti-imperialism and international communist unity. In February 1960, the Soviet First Deputy Prime Minister spoke of the unity of China and the USSR as *"unity of purpose in the struggle for socialism and communism…The unity of our ideology and social and state systems have welded firmly together our two great nations."*[251]

Years into the *"split,"* Moscow and Beijing supported the concept of mutual Sino-Soviet collaboration in the destruction of world capitalism and imperialism. The leaderships of the two great communist powers vociferously denied that any American efforts to split Moscow and Beijing would derive any great benefit for the imperialist camp. In February 1963, the Chinese Ambassador to the USSR Pan Tzu Li held a meeting with General Secretary Khrushchev. The Soviet dictator let it be known that *"I promise you that when we throw the last shovel on the grave of capitalism, we will throw it with China."* The Soviet dictator was then asked: *"Is this a beginning?"* Khrushchev then answered: *"No, not a beginning. This started a long time ago. Our parties have cooperated and will cooperate."*[252]

In the same year, the Chinese wrote a letter to the Communist Party of the Soviet Union (CPSU), where they called for the utilization of contradictions within the imperialist camp to unify the globe under the common ideology of socialism: *"The contradictions among the imperialist powers and especially those between the United States imperialism and other*

---

[249] "Summary of a conversation with the Chairman of the CC CPC (Central Committee Communist Party of China) Mao-Tse Tung" on 14 October 1959 Accessed from Cold War International History Project http://www.mtholyoke.edu/acad/intrel/maoconv.htm
[250] "Mao Zedong, Outline for a Speech on the International Situation" December 1959 Accessed From: http://digitalarchive.wilsoncenter.org/document/118893
[251] Caruthers, Osgood. "Soviet and China Celebrate Unity" <u>New York Times</u> February 14, 1960 page 12.
[252] "Soviet Display of Solidarity with China" <u>The Times (London)</u> February 16, 1963 page 8 and "Soviet-Red China Tie Still Strong, Khrushchev Says" <u>Albuquerque Tribune</u> February 15, 1963 page 1.

imperialist powers are becoming deeper and sharper and new conflicts are developing among them. In this situation, what is of decisive significance for the international cause of the proletariat as a whole is the struggle against imperialism headed by the United States and the support for the revolutionary struggles of the oppressed nations and peoples of Asia, Africa, and Latin America...It is the common desire of the people of China and the Soviet Union, of all the people in the socialist camp of the communists of all countries and of all the oppressed nations and people of the world over to strengthen the unity of the socialist camp and especially to strengthen the unity of our two parties and countries."[253]

Premier Chou En-Lai noted in 1963 that "*Some people may have thoughts of using Sino-Soviet differences to deal with China and the Soviet Union separately. Those with such ideas will certainly be disappointed. On the contrary, if any act of aggression occurs against any Socialist country this would be an act of aggression against the whole Socialist camp. It would be impossible not to give support. If a country refused to give support, it would not be a Socialist country.*"[254]

Chou also pointed out in 1964 that "*Whatever happens, the fraternal Chinese and Soviet peoples will stand together in any storm that breaks out in the world arena.*" Chou also asserted that the common interests of the USSR and China are the same and "*an objective fact and no one can deny it.*" Chou condemned Western attempts to use China against the USSR as a disgusting plot by "*reactionaries.*" He added that "*But as I see it, they had better not rejoice too soon.*" Chou noted that "*In the end, these differences will surely be resolved and the movement will be stronger and firmer as a result.*"[255]

During a celebration of the Bolshevik Revolution with Soviet officials, Chou noted that: "*The friendship and unity between the Chinese and Soviet people, based on the principles of Marxism-Leninism and proletarian internationalism, has withstood long-term tests both in years of revolution and war and in years of peaceful construction.*"[256]

On the 15th Anniversary of the signing of the Sino-Soviet Friendship, Alliance, Mutual Assistance (1965), the Soviets sent a message to the Chinese leadership stating: "*Our alliance, sealed by the treaty, is an obstacle in the way of the aggressive imperialist groups which are conducting provocations dangerous to the cause of peace and aggravating the international situation.*"[257]

In February 1965, the People's Daily of the Chinese Communist Party noted that "*Though at present there are still shadows over the relations between China and the Soviet Union no force on earth can possibly undermine the great friendship forged between our two peoples in the long years of revolutionary struggle.*"[258]

The Central Committee of the Communist Party of China noted to Khrushchev in April 1964 that "*we firmly believe that as demanded by the people of our two countries and by revolutionary people everywhere the Chinese and Soviet parties, our two countries and our two*

[253] "China Calls for Settling of Differences" The Times (London) March 14, 1963 page 9.
[254] Kellet-Long, Adam and Chipp, David. "Chou Says Sino-Soviet Ties Firm" as quoted in Congressional Record December 12, 1963 page A7572.
[255] "Chou Says Peking and Moscow Will Stand Together in a Crisis" New York Times February 4, 1964 page 2.
[256] "Mr. Chou Praises Russians" Times (London) November 8, 1960 page 12
[257] Budenz, Louis. The Bolshevik Invasion of the West (Bookmailer Linden NJ: 1966) page 75.
[258] Sleeper, Raymond. A Lexicon of Marxist-Leninist Semantics (Western Goals 1983) page 35.

peoples, will in the long run closely unite in the struggle to oppose imperialism and reaction, to uphold Marxism Leninism and proletarian internationalism, to safeguard the unity of the socialist camp and the international communist movement, to support the revolutionary movement of the oppressed peoples and nations of the world, and to defend world peace. Although at present there are differences between you and us on a number of questions of principle concerning Marxism Leninism and there is a lack of unity, we are deeply convinced that all this is only temporary. In the event of a major world crisis, the two parties, our two countries and our two peoples, will undoubtedly stand together against our common enemy. "[259]

In a communiqué issued by the Chinese Communist Party (1966), unity was promised between the PRC and USSR in case of a world war: "*The revolutionary people of the world, the great international communist movement, the great socialist camp, and the great peoples of China and the Soviet Union will eventually sweep away all obstacles and unite on the basis of Marxism-Leninism and proletarian internationalism. The Soviet people may rest assured that once the Soviet Union meets with imperialist aggression and puts up resolute resistance, China will definitely stand side by side with the Soviet Union and fight against the common enemy.* "[260]

In the 1960s, a top Moscow-based Soviet Communist Party theoretician observed how the *"decadent capitalists"* believed that the Sino-Soviet *"split"* would be their salvation. The unnamed top Soviet theoretician further stated that *"What they do not understand is that the controversy is only a debate concerning their funeral arrangements.* "[261]

The PRC also conveyed greetings on the 53rd Anniversary of the Bolshevik Revolution in 1970. The underlying tone of the Chinese message to the Soviets was ideologically muted, yet fully supportive of at least a semblance of a friendly relationship between the USSR and China: *"Differences of principle must not hinder the maintenance and development of normal state relations between two countries on the basis of the five principles of peaceful co-existence.* "[262]

The sentiment behind the Sino-Soviet public statements of solidarity was confirmed by transcripts of secret meetings between the leadership of the international communist camp of countries. In October 1964, a record of the conversation between the Soviet Ambassador to China Stepan V. Chervonenko and Mongolian Ambassador to the China Dondongiin Tsevegmid revealed that *"...Zhou Enlai spoke to the effect that the disagreements between the MPR[263] and the PRC[264] were not the main thing, the main thing was unity. Zhou Enlai cited Mao Zedong's words to the effect that socialist countries could have disagreements, but that this was a secondary question, and in the struggle against imperialism socialist countries must be united,*

---

[259] Sleeper, Raymond. A Lexicon of Marxist-Leninist Semantics (Western Goals 1983) pages 309-310.

[260] Central Committee of the Communist Party of China "Letter of the Central Committee of the Communist Party of China to the Central Committee of the Communist Party of the Soviet Union" March 22, 1966 Accessed http://www.marxists.org/history/international/comintern/sino-soviet-split/cpc/22march1966.htm

[261] Butler, Eric D. "The Fraser Kow-tow in Communist China" On Target July 2, 1976 Accessed From: http://www.alor.org/Volume12/Vol12No23.htm

[262] "Soviet Trade Unit Arrives in Peking" New York Times November 13, 1970 page 5.

[263] Mongolian People's Republic

[264] People's Republic of China

and this was the main thing. If imperialism attacked one socialist country, all socialist countries must come forward united in this struggle..."[265]

Deng Xiaoping and Romanian Communist dictator Nicolae Ceausescu echoed their support for the unity of purpose within the entire communist bloc during a future global conflict with the capitalist world:

"Comrade Nicolae Ceausescu : *Of course, we understand that in case of a war against imperialism we will have to act in common, but these actions – which require the mobilization of the whole people – must be performed on the basis of a close cooperation, with the independence of each country being observed, and the participation of each army as an independent army, as a national force. This will ensure that the effort of each country will really be an effort from all viewpoints.*

Comrade Deng Xiaoping : *We wholly agree with your opinion. We acted like that during the war in Korea. We can tell you that, together with the Korean comrades, we drew up a battle plan, but on the basis of the principles put forward by comrade Ceausescu just now. We cannot admit the fact that Vietnam and Korea be subordinated to our country because China is a bigger country. But your experience is richer than ours because you came across such problems within the framework of COMECON and of the Warsaw Treaty Organization. We know that you have fought and think that there are many people who agree with you."*[266]

KGB defector Major Anatoli Golitsyn provided anecdotal evidence illustrating that the Sino-Soviet split was deception that was contrived to allow the USSR to develop their long-range missiles, while allowing the Beijing to seek increased Western assistance and trade. KGB Chairman Alexander Shelepin explained this strategy in a lecture to an inner circle of high KGB officers in 1959. In this lecture, Shelepin allegedly explained that a contrived split could be created to provide strategic disinformation to Western audiences.[267]

Golitsyn recalled on another occasion that KGB Chairman Shelepin gave a lecture in 1958 explaining how the Soviets could use fake splits to deceive the West. The United States could then be drawn into believing that by helping one side, it could weaken the USSR. After that lecture Shelepin let it slip that China would be the perfect candidate for the deception.[268]

Golitsyn explained the alleged fake Sino-Soviet split as a part of what the KGB internally described as the *"scissors strategy."* Golitsyn recalled that the purpose of the scissors strategy was as follows: *"Duality in Sino-Soviet polemics is used to mask the nature of the goals and the*

---

[265] From the Diary of S.V. Chervonenko, Memorandum of Conversation Between Soviet Ambassador to China Stepan V. Chervonenko and Mongolian Ambassador to China Dondongiin Tsevegmid October 7, 1964 Accessed From:
http://digitalarchive.wilsoncenter.org/document/117700

[266] "Transcript of the discussions held with the delegation of the Chinese Communist Party which participated in the proceedings of the 9th Congress of the Romanian Communist Party" 26 July 1965
Accessed From the Cold War International History Project
http://wilsoncenter.org/index.cfm?topic_id=1409&fuseaction=va2.document&identifier=5034B9
D8-96B6-175C-
949D8FCA396FC2DE&sort=Collection&item=Romania%20in%20the%20Cold%20War

[267] Nyquist, J.R. "Russia and China's Secret Collusion" June 7, 1999 WorldNetDaily Accessed
http://www.worldnetdaily.com/news/article.asp?ARTICLE_ID=19727

[268] Epstein, Edward Jay. Deception (Simon & Schuster, 1989) page 97.

degree of coordination in the communist effort to achieve them. The feigned disunity of the communist world promotes real disunity in the noncommunist world. Each blade of the communist pair of scissors makes the other more effective. The militancy of one nation helps the activist detente diplomacy of the other. Mutual charges of hegemonism help to create the right climate for one or the other to negotiate agreements with the West. False alignments, formed with third parties by each side against the other, make it easier to achieve specific communist goals, such as the acquisition of advanced technology or the negotiation of arms control agreements or communist penetration of the Arab and African states. In Western eyes the military, political, economic, and ideological threat from world communism appears diminished. In consequence Western determination to resist the advance of communism is undermined. At a later stage the communist strategists are left with the option of terminating the split and adopting the strategy of 'one clenched fist.' "[269]

Golitsyn then stated that the relations between China and anti-Soviet nations would be established as a result of being deceived by the PRC-Soviet split. These Third World and Western nations would then play the *"China Card"* against the Soviets. The Chinese would then have influence in these nations and be able to acquire valuable technology from their new allies. At an opportune moment, Golitsyn then stated the secret Sino-Soviet alliance would then become open: *"In each of these the scissors strategy will play its part; probably, as the final stroke, the scissors blades will close. The element of apparent duality in Soviet and Chinese policies will disappear. The hitherto concealed coordination between them will become visible and predominant. The Soviets and the Chinese will be officially reconciled. Thus the scissors strategy will develop logically into the 'strategy of one clenched fist' to provide the foundation and driving force of a world communist federation."*[270]

Golitsyn then elaborated further: *"Before long, the communist strategists might be persuaded that the balance had swung irreversibly in their favor. In that event they might well decide on Sino-Soviet 'reconciliation.' The scissors strategy would give way to the strategy of 'one clenched fist.' At that point the shift in the political and military balance would be plain for all to see. Convergence would not be between two equal parties, but would be on terms dictated by the communist bloc. The argument for accommodation with the overwhelming strength of communism would be virtually unanswerable. Pressures would build up for changes in the American political and economic system...Traditional conservatives would be isolated and driven toward extremism. They might become the victims of a new McCarthyism of the left. The Soviet dissidents who are now extolled as heroes of the resistance to Soviet communism would play an active part in arguing for convergence. Their present supporters would be confronted with a choice of forsaking their idols or acknowledging the legitimacy of the new Soviet regime."*[271] In light of the open reconciliation of Moscow and Beijing in 1989 and their subsequent military cooperation and threats against the United States, it is very possible that we are living in the times of what Golitsyn termed *"one clenched fist."*

In 1961, former CPUSA official Jay Lovestone confirmed to the Senate Internal Security Subcommittee that Moscow and Beijing were still united in their desire to ultimately destroy the United States *"Let me say a few words about the differences between Moscow and Peiping,*

---

[269] Golitsyn, Anatoli. <u>New Lies for Old</u> (Clarion House: Atlanta GA 1984) Accessed From: http://www.spiritoftruth.org/newlies4old.pdf

[270] Ibid.

[271] Ibid.

which touches the very heart of the Communist plans for our country. In recent months, the Chinese Communist Party leadership has begun to develop some ideological differences with and grievances against the Soviet party ruling group. These differences and grievances have never been officially acknowledged or fully admitted. Nonetheless, they were there, though often exaggerated or misunderstood, especially in the non-Communist world. To the extent that there have been or still are, such differences between the Chinese and Soviet Communist Parties, they are important because of the size of Mao's organization, the area and population under its iron heel, the strategic position of the Chinese mainland, and the particular appeal which the Chinese Communist movement, being nonwhite, might have among the people of the industrially underdeveloped areas. However, in evaluating these or any other differences between Communist parties, we must, first of all, keep uppermost in our mind that whether they be rhetorical, tactical, or doctrinal differences, Communist parties are bound together by an all-important, overriding goal—and that is Communist conquest and transformation of the world, and the first prerequisite for this is the destruction of the United States…Moreover, in the specific Sino-Soviet case, the differences have not been of such a character as to eliminate, change vitally or soften in the least the hostile policies of either Moscow or Peiping toward the United States and the rest of the free world. Moscow and Peiping always have been, and are today, in full agreement on their basic aim to bury us, though they may, at one time or another, disagree over certain details of the funeral arrangements they would like to make for us. Actually, the differences between Moscow and Peiping involve not so much 'ideology' as a power struggle within the international Communist movement."[272]

Some American generals, columnists, and other anti-communists warned that the Sino-Soviet *"split"* was either a calculated deception or vastly over exaggerated by the *"powers that be"* in Washington and Wall Street in pursuit of their own profit and fulfillment of wishful thinking.

Former Trotskyite Communist-turned traditionalist conservative James Burnham predicted that the United States would take advantage of the Sino-Soviet dispute *"to continue evading the challenge of communism."* He wrote: *Internal disputes are not necessarily signs of weakness or decay."* Burnham gave the example of Islam which rapidly expanded its territorial conquests despite *"fierce and bloody internal"* divisions.[273]

Former Chairman of the Joint Chiefs of Staff Admiral Arthur W. Radford stated in 1962 that *"Red China would combine with the USSR to do the lobbying in General Assembly to get the votes needed to reorganize the U.N. for communist purposes."*[274]

According to labor columnist Victor Riesel, the Sino Soviet split was a strategic disinformation ploy to *"throw non-communist forces off their guard."* The evidence for Reisel's contention was found from information gleaned from intelligence sources in Thailand and India which pointed to joint Sino-Soviet activities in the Chinese province of Sinkiang. Riesel wrote

---

[272] United States Senate, Committee of the Judiciary. Communist and Workers' Parties Manifesto of Adopted November-December 1960 Interpretation and Analysis Accessed From: http://www.archive.org/stream/CommunistAndWorkersPartiesManifestoAdoptedNovember-december1960/Lovestone_djvu.txt

[273] Burnham, James. The War We Are In: The Last Decade and the Next (Arlington House New Rochelle New York 1967) pages 323-328.

[274] "Recognize Red China At Your Peril" On Target May 21, 1971 Accessed From: http://www.alor.org/Volume7/Vol7No18.htm

that "*There the Chinese Communists with the help of Russian technicians, Russian money and Russian material, are building a complex of roads, factories, power plants, power lines connecting Khrushchev's Russia and Mao Tse Tung's China, railroads, research centers, bomb sites, islands of industrialization, and modern cities. There the Russians created a physicist's city to help the joint efforts. There the Chinese and Soviets are exploiting huge uranium deposits.*"[275]

US Army Major General T.A. Lane (Retired) also expressed concerns in a January 20, 1965 editorial that the Sino-Soviet "*split*" was an "*opiate*" to deceive the West. General Lane explained the rationale behind the joint Chinese-Soviet deception strategy: "*It exploits the bourgeois faith in the status quo and reluctance to face reality. It employs the discipline and flexibility of communist organization…The communists, emerging from a very inferior power position and facing a long climb to parity with the democracies, needed a deception plan which would support continuous attack without ever alerting the defenses of the West. It would not do to grab a few gains and then face unyielding hostility, as Stalin did with Truman after Potsdam. The answer was the Jekyll and Hyde routine. While Mao pursued his course of terror and aggression, Khrushchev would wear the mask of the deviation who would 'reason' with the bourgeois leaders. This double image would keep the free world from focusing on the true nature and purposes of communism. It would cater to the bourgeois preconception that communist purposes could be moderated by cooperation to reach accommodation with the free world. It would provide an opiate to soothe the victim through the sequence of disasters which would attend his declining power.*"[276]

Despite popular perceptions to the contrary, the Soviets and Chinese continued to cooperate militarily. Joint statements of Sino-Soviet military solidarity were also issued in the early 1960s. As of November 1961, KGB defector Major Golitsyn reported that the KGB still provided advice to China on the physical protection of nuclear installations. He also reported that the Soviets continued to cooperate with the Chinese in building up Mao's atomic warfare potential.[277]

In 1961, the Chinese newspaper People's Daily praised the USSR for resuming nuclear bomb tests as a "*step for peace.*"[278] In 1961, Soviet Marshal Rodion Malinovsky hailed the close ties between the Soviet Army and the Chinese PLA. He called for the continued alliance of the two armies "*in the interest of defending the security of our two countries.*"[279] China also backed the East Germans in their position on the status of Berlin. Marshal Ho Lung stated to the East Germans that "*the whole of the 650,000,000 people of China stand on your side.*" Marshal Ho also added that an attack on East Germany "*is an attack on the whole Socialist camp.*"[280] Soviet Marshal Rodion Malinovsky cabled greetings to Chinese PLA Marshal Lin Biao in August 1964.[281]

---

[275] Riesel, Victor. "Cooperation Uncovered: Alleged Russia-China Rift Revealed as Hoax" Marion Star August 22, 1962 page 23.

[276] Lane, Major General (Retired) T.A. "Sino Soviet Split An Opiate" The Post Standard January 20, 1965 page 15.

[277] Elizabeth Clare Prophet. Actions Speak Louder than Words Accessed From: http://www.tslpl.org/spirit/actions.htm

[278] "Red China Backs Soviet" New York Times September 3, 1961 page 3.

[279] "Malinovsky Hails Red China's Army" New York Times August 1, 1961 page 3.

[280] "Peiping Backs Germans" New York Times October 8, 1961 page 2.

[281] "Malinovsky Hails China Army" New York Times August 2, 1964 page 38.

According to a SIPRI study, the USSR exported weapons for the Chinese Armed Forces even after the "*split*" of 1960. Military hardware shipped to China from the USSR in this period included IL-18 transport planes, MIG-21 fighters, SS C-2b coastal defense missiles, SS-N-2 Styx naval missiles, Komar fast attack craft, Osa I Class missile boats, Romeo class submarines, SA-2 SAMs, P-6 fast attack craft, Golf and Whiskey class submarines, and T-43 Class minesweepers.[282]

Sometimes the Red Chinese colluded with their Eastern European allies to spy on NATO targets. Why would China, all the way in East Asia, even desire intelligence on NATO targets? Would it be possible that the Chinese and Albanians transmitted this information to Moscow through secret channels that were undetected and unknown by the CIA? In 1961, Italian intelligence arrested Albanian agent Kallco Koko in Rome and at least 6 Chinese agents for spying on NATO installations.[283]

The Soviets and their Eastern European allies also maintained close technical relations with China's nuclear weapons industry in the 1960s. China continued its relationships with nuclear scientists in Eastern Europe after 1959. For example, Klaus Fuchs met with Qian Sanqiang in East Germany and gave him numerous documents which sped up Chinese atomic weapons research.[284]

The Times of London reported in 1976 that the Chinese also utilized precision equipment from Czechoslovakia and East Germany to assist in the construction in their atomic bomb programs of the 1960s and 1970s.[285]

When Swiss businessmen were being pursued for their illegal shipments of cobalt to China, they fled to Eastern European countries. The shipments of cobalt were destined for Beijing's nuclear bomb program and the material was shipped through Germany and Czechoslovakia and then onto China. It should be noted that cobalt in atomic bombs would serve to greatly enhance the firepower and destructive capacity of such weapons. Despite the split, it is interesting to observe that such collaborators with China found it comfortably convenient to use Eastern European countries as conduits for the transferring of sensitive atomic bomb technology and materials to China.[286]

The Chinese were also still considered potential recipients for Soviet-made ballistic missiles well after the official "*split*" of 1960. A North Korean Colonel reported in 1963 that: "*the Soviet Union has powerful missiles, that probably these missiles are also stationed in the Far East, but it would be better and quieter if the Soviet Union gave such missiles to the DPRK and to the Chinese.*"[287]

[282] Kim, Taeho and Gill, Bates. China's Arms Acquisitions from Abroad: A Quest for Superb and Secret Weapons (SIPRI-Oxford University Press 1995) See Appendix Accessed From: http://books.sipri.org/files/RR/SIPRIRR11.pdf
[283] Faligot, Roger. The Chinese Secret Service (Morrow, 1989) page 284.
[284] Ibid, page 258.
[285] Peiris, Denzil. "Accelerated Development of Nuclear Weapons" The Times (London) September 28, 1976 page 9 and Minor, Michael S. "China's Nuclear Development Program" Asian Survey June 1976 page 575.
[286] "Bomb Aid to China Linked to 2 Swiss; Cobalt Deals Cited" New York Times July 16, 1965 page 4.
[287] "Conversation between Soviet Ambassador in North Korea Vasily Moskovsky and Czechoslovak Ambassador Moravec" April 15, 1963 Accessed from Cold War International

Soviet bloc states were also considered by the Chinese to be intermediaries in the provisioning of nuclear weapons technology for Beijing. In August 1963, Soviet Ambassador in North Korea Vasily Moskovsky noted that *"(I) received the GDR Ambassador at his request. (The ambassador) said that the Koreans, apparently on Chinese instructions, are asking whether they could obtain any kind of information about nuclear weapons and the atomic industry from German universities and research institutes."*[288]

National security scholar Dr. Joseph D. Douglass reported in an essay on POW-MIA affairs that Czechoslovakia proposed joint cooperation with China on medical experimentation on American POWs captured during the Vietnam War: *"...a senior Czech military intelligence officer who was undercover in China as a military attaché reported on a Chinese request to share information on continued medical test programs. The Chinese official complained to the Czech 'attaché' that even if there were developing antagonisms between their two countries, some cooperative activities should continue, for example, he suggested, the joint research on American POWs. We are continuing this research, he said, and asked, why don't we continue to share results of this research? There is no reason to keep your program secret. We know the American POWs are being sent to the Soviet Union for research. Information exchange on these research programs would be of use to both our countries."*[289]

Columnist Henry J. Taylor believed that the Soviets and Chinese cooperated through North Korea in masterminding the hijacking of the American ship Pueblo. He noted that *"Moscow-Peking ideological differences notwithstanding, the intelligence coordination continues between the Soviets and the Teh Wu in Peking and Pyongyang. Washington keeps our public ignorant of this by our officials' Soviet cover-up policy, which is a systemized public relations pitch to make it appear to our public that by Washington's statesmanship our relations with the USSR have improved."*[290]

Various Soviet allies cooperated with China in smuggling drugs to the West in an effort to demoralize the capitalist world and to generate additional hard currencies. Opium grown and processed in northern China was shipped to North Korea, then East Germany and then to Western Europe. Shipments from China via North Korea were also sent to Albania, Cuba, and various African nations.[291]

The Soviets and their allies continued their trade relations with China throughout the 1960s and early 1970s. Many of the Soviet exports to China during this period included dual-use technologies which could be incorporated in Beijing's defense industries. A large proportion of

History Project Accessed From:
http://wilsoncenter.org/index.cfm?topic_id=1409&fuseaction=va2.document&identifier=666C18 41-DF40-D7B1- A96259481D90F2CD&sort=Coverage&item=Korea,%20Democratic%20People's%20Republic %20of,%20(DPRK),%20North%20Korea
[288] Conversation between Soviet Ambassador in North Korea Vasily Moskovsky and the German Ambassador 26 August 1963 Accessed From: http://digitalarchive.wilsoncenter.org/document/110608
[289] Douglass, Dr. Joseph D. "Malfeasance in the Search for American POW/MIAs" Accessed from http://www.aiipowmia.com/reports/dglssmalfe.html
[290] Taylor, Henry J. "Behind the Pueblo Affair: How Red China and USSR Coordinate Espionage" Human Events March 2, 1968 page 12.
[291] A.H. Stanton Candlin. Psycho-Chemical Warfare (Arlington House 1974) pages 105-106.

this Soviet-Chinese trade was conducted on a barter basis. Some were also luxuries for the CCP leadership. Mao received a new train from East Germany in the early 1960s, which was equipped with every luxury, including air conditioning, lighting, hot, running water, living rooms, and appliances.[292]

In 1965, the Soviets and Chinese concluded a trade agreement, where Moscow would export machine tools, passenger planes, helicopters, vehicles, tractors, metals, lumber, chemicals, and industrial equipment to Beijing. China was to supply garments, silk, apples, citrus fruits, shoes, pork, chemicals, nonferrous metals, and livestock products to the Soviets.[293]

In 1972, China received two IL-62 airliners from the Soviets, as a result of a trade agreement concluded in 1970.[294] China concluded a trade agreement with the Soviet Union in 1964, where Moscow would export tractors, petroleum products, trucks, industrial chemicals, and IL-18 transport planes to China.[295]

Trade in 1972 between the USSR and China totaled $290.4 million and consisted of Soviet exports of turbine generators, trucks, helicopters, airplane spare parts, lathes, cars, tractors, and machinery spare parts to the Maoist regime. The Soviets imported non-ferrous metals, high grade ores, fuel derived from animal fats, fruit, knitwear, furs, yard-goods, and vacuum flasks from China.[296]

During the "Sino-Soviet split," Poland continued to export coal enrichment machinery and power generators to China. Romania exported drilling rigs, refinery equipment, oil pipeline, and electric power equipment to China. In 1969, Romania also participated in the design of the Peking General Petrochemical Works, while Czechoslovakia refined Chinese uranium in 1965. In the period from 1965 to 1975, China assisted Albania with the development of oil refineries, oil processing plants, and electric power plants. China also possibly sold Romania a refinery during this period. Meanwhile, China imported crude oil and petrochemicals from Albania, Romania, and Poland. Starting in 1969, China also reportedly imported oil from Yugoslavia.[297]

During the 1960s and early 1970s, the Soviet and Chinese positions towards various civil conflicts and leftist regimes in the Third World coincided on more occasions than not. The evidence mentioned in the following paragraphs seemed to validate the veracity of the public and secret Sino-Soviet assertions that the two communist powers would cooperate in the effort to promote world revolution. By the mid-1960s, China exported arms to communist North Vietnam, Tanzania, and the Congo People's Republic. Soviet satellite Somalia received 12 Type 62 tanks in 1970, while North Vietnam received 100 Type 62s in 1971. China also exported fifty Type 56 tanks to North Vietnam in the period 1960-1962. North Vietnam and Albania received all types of Chinese artillery in the 1960s, such field guns, anti-tank guns, multiple rocket launchers, and mortars.[298]

---

[292] Zhisui, Dr. Li. The Private Life of Chairman Mao (Random House Publishing Group 2011) page 129.
[293] "Moscow and Peking Sign '65 Trade Pact" New York Times April 30, 1965 page 2
[294] "Chinese Airline Is Said to Get Soviet Jets" New York Times February 9, 1972 page 4.
[295] "Peking to Purchase Airliners in Soviet" New York Times May 18, 1964 page 9.
[296] Durdin, Tillman. "Moscow Trading with Peking Rises" New York Times August 13, 1972 page 8.
[297] Woodard, Kim. The International Energy Relations of China (Stanford University Press, 1980) pages 67-69.
[298] Gilks, Anne and Segal, Gerald. China and the Arms Trade (Croom Helm, 1985) pages 64-69.

Former Cuban Army Captain Angel Saavedra Correa reported that Cuban intelligence (G-2) agents who secretly served at their Embassy in Washington DC passed data to both the Soviets and Chinese that was collected through espionage actions within the United States. He served as the Cuban Embassy's Air and Military Attaché until his defection in early 1960.[299] By the end of 1959 Cuba's guerrilla training camps hosted Soviet *technical advisers* while Red Chinese officers were concurrently stationed at the Minas del Frio camp.[300] In May 1959, Chinese intelligence experts secretly entered Cuba. G-2 agents under Soviet and Chinese direction entered the locals of the Cuban Confederation of Labor (CTC) and seized control over the union.[301] Former American Ambassador to Cuba Robert C. Hill reported that *"Agents coming from Moscow and some from China go back and forth between the Soviet Embassies in Mexico and Cuba."* The 56th Division of the Chinese PLA was located in the vicinity Tacajo sugar mill in Oriente Province.[302] A purser for the state-owned Cubana Airlines Salvador del Pino recalled that *"Of those coming to Cuba from Prague, 90% are military men from North Vietnam and Red China."*[303] Paul Bethel noted that *"...the Russians supplied Red China with transport in the form of 18 four engined Ilyushin turboprop aircraft for the stated purpose of transporting cargo and passengers between China and Cuba, thus making highly suspect the claims coming out of Washington that the Russians and Chinese were at odds over communist policy toward Cuba. Actually Russia shares Cuba's 43 guerrilla camps with the Red Chinese, the better to advance the subversion of Africa."* Cuba also hosted a terrorist training camp called Patrice Lumumba located on the Isle of Pines. This camp was staffed by Viet Cong guerrilla instructors, while overall direction and political instruction was supplied by Red Chinese officers. The Congolese (Zairean) communist rebel leader Gaston Soumialot visited Cuba in August 1964 and was met by resident Soviet and Chinese embassy officials. He toured terrorist training camps and secretly met with Fidel Castro, the Soviet and Chinese Ambassadors, and Nguyen Van Tien, the Permanent Representative of North Vietnam in Cuba. Senegalese leftists were among the Africans who received such training in Cuba by Chinese and Viet Cong advisers.[304]

China provided Indonesia army troops in 1964 with weapons, while supplying arms to the PKI in 1965. Such supplies comprised a grand total of 25,000 arms to Sukarno loyalists. In early 1965, a high level Indonesian political and military delegation returned from Peking with a pledge to *"strengthen their contacts in the military field."*[305] During the Sukarno period, it should be pointed out that Moscow heavily equipped the Indonesian army with weapons and training.

The Presidential Guard in pro-Moscow Ghana hosted Soviet, Chinese, and Egyptian communist advisers under the command of Soviet Colonel Zanlegu.[306] The Chinese also dispatched advisers to the communist state of Ghana under the dictatorial president Kwame Nkrumah. Colonel Yen Leng set up a training camp in Ghana, alongside East German Ministry

[299] May, Donald. "Cuban Spy Activity in US Aired" Cedar Rapids Gazette January 7, 1961 page 1.
[300] Bethel, Paul D. The Losers (Arlington House, 1969) pages 208-209.
[301] Ibid, page 174.
[302] Ibid, pages 252-253.
[303] Ibid, page 420.
[304] Ibid, pages 420-421.
[305] Gilks, Anne and Segal, Gerald. China and the Arms Trade (Croom Helm, 1985) page 43.
[306] Metrowich, F.R. Africa and Communism (Voortrekkerpers, 1967) Accessed From: http://www.rhodesia.nl/Africa%20and%20Communism.pdf

of State Security (Stasi) and Soviet personnel. These camps trained Ghanaian agents and African leftists whose ultimate aim was a Socialist United Africa under one *"Continental Union Government."*[307]

The Rhodesian police and army captured weapons from the communist forces of ZAPU/ZANU in the Wankie region of Rhodesia in 1967. Weapons formerly in the possession of the ZAPU-ZANU forces included Chinese, Soviet, and Czech rifles, bazookas, hand grenades, and explosives. Many of these arms were channeled via the OAU.[308] The main Mozambican Frelimo training camp in Tanzania also hosted Cuban and Chinese instructors. Frelimo also trained with the Soviet and Chinese-backed Tanzanian Army.[309]

During 1967, Chinese-made AK-47s were captured by the Israeli Defense Forces (IDF) from PLO stores in the Gaza Strip. Other captured Chinese-made weapons included mines, explosives, hand grenades, machine guns, and rockets.[310] By 1965, Chinese PLA officers were attached to the Syrian Army and trained PLO guerrillas. A PLO Mission was opened in Beijing in 1966, while at the same time, PLO officers were trained in Red China. In 1970, a delegation of the pro-Soviet Popular Front for the Liberation of Oman and the Arabian Gulf (PFLOAG) members visited China for continued military and political support.[311]

Since 1964, China provided the PLO with weapons and training. Between 1965 and 1969, the Chinese sent over $5 million in aid to the pro-Moscow PLO factions called the Popular Front for the Liberation of Palestine (PFLP) and the Democratic Front for the Liberation of Palestine (DFLP). Furthermore, the DFLP received training in China itself. In late 1970, Chinese army engineers were dispatched to the Soviet satellite state of South Yemen, where they collaborated with the Soviets, East Germans, and Cubans in the construction of military-economic infrastructure. By 1972, China dumped a massive amount of firearms into Fatah arsenals via ports in Baathist Iraq, Qaddafi's Libya, Baathist Syria, and Lebanon. Witnesses also alleged that Chinese PLA troops were stationed at PFLP camps in Beirut, South Yemen, and Baalbeck.[312]

A PFLOAG defector named Ahmed Deblaan traveled to pro-Soviet South Yemen in 1968 and flew to Karachi (Pakistan) on Middle East Airways. Deblaan then flew to Shanghai on Pakistan Airways and thence to Beijing on Chinese Airways. They were lodged at luxury hotels and toured historical sites within Red China. The PFLOAG terrorists were trained at a school alongside North Koreans and Africans. They were trained to utilize artillery, rockets, and small arms.

Soviet, Algerian, Chinese, and Egyptian ships ferried arms to African leftist terrorists at the port of Ponte Noire. The training camp Tlemcen (located in Algeria) trained Angolan communist MPLA cadres under the control of military personnel from Algeria, East Germany,

[307] Garrison, Lloyd. "Ghana Uncovers African Spy Network Set Up By Nkrumah With Red Aid." New York Times June 10, 1966 page 20.

[308] Gilks, Anne and Segal, Gerald. China and the Arms Trade (Croom Helm, 1985) pages 45-46.

[309] Greig, Ian. The Communist Challenge to Africa (Foreign Affairs Publishing Co., 1977) page 163.

[310] Gilks, Anne and Segal, Gerald. China and the Arms Trade (Croom Helm, 1985) pages 41-42.

[311] Greig, Ian. Subversion (Tom Stacey, 1973) pages 152-153.

[312] McForan, Desmond. The World Held Hostage (Oak-Tree Books, 1986) pages 200-201.

Cuba, China, and various, experienced liberation movements.[313] Starting in 1965, separatist terrorists in British Aden received Soviet, East German, Chinese, and Czechoslovak arms from unknown sources.[314]

As late as 1963, it was reported that the Communist Party of China paid $2 million to the Soviet International Fund of Left Wing Workers Organizations.[315] After 1963, no known Chinese contributions were made to the Fund. It is significant to point out that infusions of hard currency from Red China for this Soviet fund continued three years after the Sino-Soviet *"split"* started in 1960.

The Chinese continued to support communist parties that were sympathetic to Mao's dictatorship. However, Beijing maintained ties to communist parties and *"liberation"* movements that were also aligned with Moscow. In 1969, the 9th Congress of the CCP was attended by delegations from parties that were both loyal to Moscow and Beijing: the Romanian Communist Party, Albanian Workers Party, Workers Party of Vietnam, NLF/Vietcong of South Vietnam, and the pro-Maoist communist parties from Burma, Thailand, Malaysia, and Indonesia. Splinter Marxist-Leninist parties from San Marino, Yugoslavia, Poland, and Hungary also attended.[316]

It was known that the Chinese intelligence services were involved in supporting or guiding various American radical and communist groups. Despite the Sino-Soviet *"split,"* Leibel Bergman traveled, along with his two sons, to China via Moscow in 1965. This may have indicated either Chinese-Soviet coordination or acquiescence in support for the American New Left and Communist movements. He then met with his contact in Chinese intelligence and then relocated back to the United States in 1967. Leibel was ordered to advance the struggle against American imperialism from within the United States by networking with likeminded revolutionaries for subversive and terrorist actions. Leibel was to send other prospective American communists to China for training in espionage and other clandestine trades that would then be utilized for actions against capitalism in the United States. Some of Leibel's contacts became involved in the terrorist Weather Underground Organization (WUO).[317]

The Chinese and Soviets also were on the same side in supporting the North Vietnamese and Vietcong during the Vietnam War. In 1966, it was reported that Cuban ships were involved in loading up weapons in Chinese ports and shipping them to their mutual ally, North Vietnam.[318] In 1972, it was reported that two East German freighters were loaded with supplies and heavy trucks for North Vietnam at the Chinese port of Whampoa.[319]

In April 1965, it was reported that the Chinese ceased erecting obstacles to the Soviets transshipping missiles and other weapons through China to North Vietnam.[320] During the 1972

---

[313] Greig, Ian. The Communist Challenge to Africa (Foreign Affairs Publishing Co., 1977) pages 143-147.

[314] Greig, Ian. The Assault on the West (Foreign Affairs Publishing Company, 1968) page 143.

[315] Crozier, Brian. The Rise and Fall of the Soviet Empire (Forum 1999) page 557.

[316] Faligot, Roger. The Chinese Secret Service (Morrow, 1989) page 383.

[317] Rees, John "The Selling of a Brutal Tyranny: Red China" American Opinion May 1981 pages 7-94.

[318] "Defector Says Cuban Ships Take Chinese Arms to Hanoi" New York Times January 23, 1966 page 66.

[319] "Ships Said to Go to China" New York Times May 31, 1972 page 2.

[320] "China Said to Be Letting in Arms" The Times (London) April 8, 1965 page 12.

American naval blockade of North Vietnamese ports, China allowed the Soviets to ship war material via their rail networks to North Vietnam. A North Vietnamese delegation that consisted of Brig. Phan Trong, the Minister of Communications, and Ly Bay, the Deputy Minister of Foreign Trade, traveled to China to coordinate the joint Chinese-Soviet deliveries.[321] The NSA produced intercepts which revealed that Soviet intelligence intercepted data on American bombers through space satellites and relayed this information to Chinese intelligence. This intelligence was then passed from the Chinese to the North Vietnamese.[322]

The Sinologist Professor David N. Rowe noted in testimony to the National Committee to Restore Internal Security (November 1981) that the Soviets and the Chinese were allies in the effort to provide weapons, oil, and troops to North Vietnam. Rowe summarized the coalescence of the interests of Moscow and Beijing during the Vietnam War when he stated that: *"...when it comes down to facing up to a mutual enemy, the United States, they (USSR and China) don't feud; they cooperate, and they will continue to do so in my opinion."*[323]

Even the spirit behind the American *"opening"* to China was taken advantage of by the Maoist leadership in the interests of expanding communism in Indochina. Even worse, there were some indications that the American government covered up the diversion of grain shipments from China to North Vietnam. US intelligence reports from 1974 noted that American grain shipped to Red China was allegedly diverted to North Vietnam, which was in the process of attempting to conquer South Vietnam. The Director of the US Mission to China Armstrong was concerned that *"We are raising this matter with you now because we believe that any diversion of US grain to North Vietnam could very likely become public knowledge and could create problems which would impair trade relations between the United States and the People's Republic of China."*[324]

The Soviets and their satraps in the Communist Party USA also actively campaigned for Beijing's admission to the United Nations as the sole representative of China. In September 1971, the USSR made it clear that they opposed the original American plan for admitting Taiwan and the People's Republic to the UN. Pravda noted *"Of great significance in raising the effectiveness and authority of the United Nations would be achievement of a genuine universality. This would be fostered by the restoration of the legitimate rights of the Chinese People's Republic in the United Nations and the expulsion of the Chiang Kai-shekists."*[325]

In October 1971, Soviet UN Ambassador Yakov Malik noted that the two China policy was an *"unsavory policy intended to sever Taiwan from the People's Republic of China."* Malik added that the United States tried to *"frighten the members of the United Nations"* by opposing

[321] "Russian Arms Sent Across China by Rail to Beat the American Blockade of N. Vietnam" Times (London) May 19, 1972 page 6.

[322] Epstein, Edward Jay. Deception (Simon & Schuster, 1989) page 97.

[323] Morris, Robert. Our Globe Under Siege III (J&W Enterprises: Mantoloking NJ 1988) pages 21-22.

[324] Declassified Document Department of State July 17, 1974 Accessed From: http://www.wikileaks.org/plusd/cables/1974STATE155129_b.html

[325] Shabad, Theodore. "Soviet Firm in Opposing 2-China Plan" New York Times September 22, 1971 page 4.

the expulsion of the Taiwanese. Malik stated that the American position was also *"absurd inventions and ridiculous fairy tales composed for children of preschool age."*[326]

In 1971, the Soviets voted for China's admission into the UN and the ejection of Taiwan. Izvestia noted that the admission of the PRC to the UN was a *"triumph for common sense."* Izvestia further noted that *"Through all the general Assembly session at which the question of restoring the rights of China was debated, the position of the Soviet Union remained principles constant and unchanged. No matter how our relations with the Chinese leader evolved-as is known they have deteriorated through no fault of our own-the Soviet Union, true to the internationalist principles of its Leninist foreign policy always proceeded from the fact that the Chinese people could not be ignored and had to be represented in the United Nations."*[327]

In 1971, the Chairman of the Communist Party USA (CPUSA) Gus Hall stated in an interview with communist writers in New York that Nixon's opening to Beijing was a *"break in the wall"* that the United States originally imposed around Red China. Hall stated *"We not only welcome these minimal moves by US imperialism but these are the very things we've been fighting for, regardless of what the intentions of the US imperialists are. It's a break in the wall that the US has tried to build up. We welcome the small shift on US trade policy, the lifting of restrictions on newsmen, and on the use of passports generally, the lifting of restrictions on shipping and the other steps that have been taken. These are very important steps in breaking the US blockade of China...However, they must be seen only as a very minimal beginning. To be meaningful the next step will have to be to end the US blockade of People's China in the United Nations and an end to the 'two Chinas policy.' The US will have to withdraw all its troops and personnel from Taiwan and withdraw the Seventh Fleet from the Taiwan Straits and Gulf of Tonkin."*[328]

Various classified documents that were leaked to the Taiwanese hinted at Red China's continued adherence to the *"Marxist camp"* and an unwillingness to completely align with the United States against the Soviet Union. Chou En-lai noted in his March 1973 Report on the International Situation that: ***"We cannot propose to unite with the US to oppose the USSR, though we share the same views with the US on certain issues***.*"*[329]

Deng Xiaoping noted in a speech on July 20, 1977 (Third Plenary Session of the 10th Congress of the CCP) that: *"In the international united front struggle the most important strategy is unification as well as struggle. That is to say, to obtain unification through struggle and to develop struggle through unification. Isn't this a form of contradiction? Actually, it is not. This is Mao Tse Tung's great discovery which has unlimited power. Even though the American imperialists can be said to be number one nation in scientific and technical matters, she knows absolutely nothing in this area. In the future she will have no way of avoiding defeat by our hands...**We belong to the Marxist Camp and can never be so thoughtless that we cannot distinguish friends from enemies**. **Nixon, Ford, Carter, and future American imperialistic leaders all fall into this category (enemies). They want to use the split between us and the***

[326] Tanner, Henry. "Russian Derides US Plan on China" New York Times October 21, 1971 page 1.
[327] "Soviet, in First Comment, Hails UN Vote on China" New York Times October 26, 1971 page 14.
[328] Scott, Paul. "Kremlin Approves US-Red China Ties" Lewiston Daily May 18, 1971 page 13.
[329] Classified Chinese Communist Documents: A Selection (Institute for International Relations: National Chengchi University Republic of China 1978) page 491.

USSR to destroy the world socialist system in order to manipulate and lessen the Soviet threat toward themselves. Why can't we take advantage of the contradiction and grudge that exists between them and initiate actions that would be favorable to our national policy? We must control others and cannot allow others to control us. We cannot be our master if we overly rely on others and do not take the initiative. This will definitely not happen to us. We must seize all opportunities to acquire things that we need under conditions set forth by us. What we need mainly is scientific and technical knowledge and equipment. This would contribute the most to our modernization plans. At the same time, improvement in China-USA relations is inevitable and as and as this relationship develops the American imperialists will defer to our wishes. Once normalization between China and the USA is finalized it will naturally be beneficial to us in resolving the problem of liberating Taiwan. After that the sources of all of our internal problems will vanish and even the confused and complicated issues of Tibet and Sinkiang will also be resolved. Many American imperialists have been rushing to our country, including two Presidents, two Secretaries of State, Congressman, and also other influential military and political figures. Even Vance can hardly wait to visit us next month."[330]*

The Soviets were also interested in revamping their economy and attracting even more investment and technology from the West and the United States. Moscow was keenly interested in the successes and structure of China's Special Economic Zones as a tool for increasing its imports of high technology and industrial goods from the capitalist world. Various Soviet bloc delegations visited the Shenzhen Special Economic Zone. During the 1980s, there were also some indications that Deng Xiaoping, Chen Yun, and Hu Qiamou all supported the maintenance or expansion of relations with the USSR: *"The Shenzhen special economic zone has not only drawn the attention of the entire nation, but also produced worldwide reaction. Economic delegations from the Soviet Union, Hungary and Korea have visited Shenzhen. Kim Chong-il, son of Korean strong man Kim Il-sung, has also visited Shenzhen...Hu Qiaomu and Chen Yun hold identical views with regard to China's policy towards the Soviet Union. Hu Qiaomu formally suggested an early improvement of Sino-Soviet relations. But Deng Xiaoping maintained that China should keep the Soviet Union at a certain distance while improving relations with it. He is resolutely opposed to taking the Soviet road."[331]*

Both official Soviet and Chinese sources supported the improvement in relations between Moscow and Beijing as a means of consolidating the international united front of communist bloc states. The Hong Kong newspaper Wen Wei Po noted in 1983 that *"there has been a trend for relations between China and pro-Soviet countries to get gradually warmer."[332]* A Radio Peace and Progress broadcast in the same year noted that *"even in the most complicated periods, the CPSU and the Soviet government have never forgotten that the long range and fundamental interests of the Soviet Union and China are identical.*"[333] In January 1983, the Soviet-controlled radio station called the 1st August Radio noted that the *"signs had begun to*

---

[330] Teng Hsiao-ping Speech Behind the Scenes of Red China's Foreign Policy The Chan Wang Publication Service September 30, 1978 pages 1-5.

[331] "Hongkong Journal on Disagreements Between Deng Xiaoping, Chen Yun and Deng Liqun" Cheng Ming June 9, 1984

[332] "Hong Kong Paper Notes Soviet Bloc's Gestures Towards China" BBC Summary of World Broadcasts October 13, 1983

[333] "The USSR's Wish to Improve Relations with China" Radio Peace and Progress January 3, 1983

appear that the dark clouds over Sino-Soviet relations might vanish, noting that, in the past year and more, the two countries had shared basically identical views on a series of international issues. Both had supported Argentina in its struggle against British colonialism and the Arab people in their struggle against Israeli aggression; China had officially recognized the Angolan government and no longer supported the Solidarity trade union, and has given official support to the solemn stand of the Polish government; and the Soviet government fully supported China's stand on the Taiwan question. In a word, said the radio, there is a basis for improving the relations between the two countries. The question now is whether the two sides have the sincerity to do so.[334] Radio Peace and Progress noted in 1985 that ***"Both the USSR and Vietnam have linked the task of improving their relations with the PRC with the task of developing their relations with all socialist countries. This shows the communists' class strategy, which aims at further strengthening solidarity among all socialist forces in the world so that the anti-imperialist united front can be consolidated. Under the present circumstances, such solidarity is particularly essential***.*"*[335]

Even by the 1980s, there can be no doubt that the continued, underlying goal of Soviet and Chinese foreign policies was the communization of the globe. In 1984, North Korean President Kim Il-sung and SED Chairman Erich Honecker engaged in a discussion concerning foreign policies. It appeared that this conversation provided proof that the Chinese *"opening"* to the United States was an effort to absorb massive amounts of technology. The rhetoric which mentioned alleged Soviet revisionism was either deceptive balderdash whose significance was vastly overstated by Western policy making elites. The North Korean dictator expressed that *"Given the complex world situation, I hope that the Soviet Union and China work things out. I believe that the development of relations with the US is not targeted against the Soviet Union. Mao Zedong and Zhou En-lai already told me that when they established relations with the US. They told us every time they met with Japan and the US. The only objective of these relations is to obtain developed technology and credit from Japan and the US. Deng Xiaoping is said to have stated in the US that the arms build-up in the US is good for peace. I don't know if that's so. This is the first time I have heard of Deng Xiaoping expressing a sentiment like that."*[336]

The Chinese privately expressed their vociferous opposition to President Reagan for real and alleged American actions in support for Taiwan, South Korea, South Africa, and Israel. In a 1984 meeting with former President Reagan, Deng Xiaoping and Zhao Ziyang noted that *"the United States had seriously offended others in supporting the four 'unsinkable aircraft carriers' in the world (namely Taiwan, South Korea, Israel, and South Africa) and voiced his hope that the United States would revise its policy. The United States still wants to support the 'four unsinkable aircraft carriers.'"*[337]

---

[334] "1st August Radio Sees a Basis for Improving Sino-Soviet Relations" 1st August Radio January 21, 1983

[335] "USSR and Vietnam Want Improved Relations with China" Radio Peace and Progress July 10, 1985

[336] Memorandum of conversation between Erich Honecker and Kim Il Sung, 31 May 1984. on the meeting between Erich Honecker and Kim Il Sung on 31 May 1984 Accessed From Cold War International History Project Database http://www.wilsoncenter.org/topics/pubs/ACF2837.pdf

[337] "Hong Kong Journal Reviews Reagan's China Visit: Assassination Plot" Cheng Ming June 6, 1984

Cheng Ming also admitted that Moscow and Beijing engaged in deception to divert American attention away from the growing outward relations between the two main communist powers: *"When Chinese Vice-Foreign Minister Qian Qichen visited the Soviet Union, Gromyko asked Qian privately: Does China truly believe the sweet words and honeyed phrases of the imperialists? Qian answered: China has been dealing with imperialists for more than 100 years, it clearly understands the essence of imperialism. Gromyko expressed his desire to develop relations between the Soviet Union and China. Qian said that the two countries could develop their economic relations. **People notice that although Sino-Soviet relations are steadily improving, the Soviet Press has not eased its attacks on China. Why? There are two reasons for this: (1) Diverting the attention of the United States from the improvement of Sino-Soviet relations;** (2) Quelling the desires of the East European countries to improve their relations with China."*[338]

Various Soviet and Eastern European communist dictators also believed in the great benefit of expanded cooperation between Moscow and Beijing. Ceausescu remarked that *"Romania should make a substantial increase in its contribution to the defense not only of the Warsaw Pact but also of Peking and the whole communist world."*[339] In November 1985, Gorbachev himself noted *"We need to wage our struggle for China patiently and persistently, for a rapprochement with it. This is very important from the point of view of (our) country's prospects..."*[340]

East German dictator Erich Honecker asserted in 1985 that *"We are following the foreign policy of the People's Republic of China in the international arena with great attention. **In our opinion, some of the PRC's steps, such as the most recent Chinese comments on strengthening world peace and disarmament, offer new possibilities for an active political dialogue**. At the same time, we do not overlook the fact that differences of opinion remain and that the Chinese continue to insist on their conditions with respect to the Soviet Union. **We are using our recently-developed contacts to the PRC to strengthen positions in Chinese foreign policy that allow for parallel or analogous action regarding the major issue of our time, the defense of world peace**. We have, among other things, confirmed our interest in developing normal, fruitful relations by concluding a long-term trade and payments agreement. Progress down this road is to the advantage of both states and does not represent a disadvantage any third parties."*[341]

The Chinese continued to hold Soviet-style parades on the anniversaries of the conquest of that country by Mao's forces. Pro-Chinese, along with Soviet-line, leftist and communist rulers and parties were in attendance at the anniversary parades of the conquest of China by Mao's forces. In October 1984, the Red Chinese National Day parade was attended by Prince Sihanouk, top officials of the Khmer Rouge, pro-Chinese Vietnamese Communist Party leader Hoang Van Hoan, Betty Kaunda, wife of the pro-Soviet Zambian President Kenneth Kaunda, and Juan Antonio Samaranch, President of the International Olympic Committee. The foreign

---

[338] "Hong Kong Journal Reviews Reagan's China Visit: Assassination Plot" Cheng Ming June 6, 1984

[339] Pacepa. Ion. Red Horizons (Regnery Washington DC 1990) page 8.

[340] 28 November 1985 Conference at the CC CPSU on preparation for the XXVII Congress of the CPSU Accessed From: http://www2.gwu.edu/~nsarchiv/NSAEBB/NSAEBB172/Doc27.pdf

[341] "Speech by Comrade Erich Honecker" October 22, 1985 Parallel History Project on Cooperative Security Accessed From:http://www.php.isn.ethz.ch/collections/colltopic.cfm?lng=en&id=19114&navinfo=14465

delegations and the top Chinese Communist Party leadership reviewed 6,000 militia, police, and PLA troops that marched by the reviewing stands. Tanks, trucks, armored vehicles, jeeps, anti-tank, ballistic missiles, multiple rocket launchers, jet fighters, and bombers also passed the reviewing stands. Portraits of Marx, Engels, Lenin, and Stalin were present at the parade.[342]

Many Soviet bloc and allied states also issued congratulatory telegrams to the CCP leadership on the founding of the so-called People's Republic. In October 1984, North Korea, Romania, Yugoslavia, Democratic Kampuchea, Pakistan, Bangladesh, Poland, Hungary, and East Germany congratulated Red China on its National Day.[343] In October 1984, Albanian communist ruler Ramiz Alia transmitted greetings to Red Chinese President Li Xiannian, which wished for *"well-being and prosperity"* of the *"Chinese people."* Bulgarian communist leaders Todor Zhivkov and Grisha Filipov lauded how *"bilateral relations contributed to the economic and cultural development of the two countries."* Czech communist leaders Gustav Husak, Lubomir Strougal and Bohuslav Chnoupek supported *"further beneficial development of relations"* between Czechoslovakia and China. East German SED leaders Erich Honecker, Willi Stoph, and Horst Sindermann noted that *"in China's struggle against imperialism, a traditional friendship had developed and that its further development was a contribution to the securing of peace."* Romanian communist leaders Nicolae Ceausescu and Constantin Dascalescu extolled the *"friendship, solidarity and fruitful co-operation between the two Parties and countries."* Yugoslav communists Veselin Djuranovic, Ali Sukrija, and Milka Planinc *"expressed confidence in the further successful development of relations."* The Hungarian communist newspaper <u>Nepszabadsag</u> praised the *"incomparable assistance of the socialist countries, first of all the Soviet Union, in China's struggle."* Polish communist leaders Henryk Jablonski and Wojciech Jaruzelski noted that *"Poland wished to make permanent and expand mutually beneficial co-operation"* with China. The Polish communist newspaper <u>Trybuna Ludu</u> noted that *"that China's relations with the socialist countries were developing favourably, especially in trade, despite the lack of convergence of views on some vital political issues."*[344]

In early October 1989, the representatives of East and West, multinational corporations and communists, all converged in China to celebrate the 40th Anniversary of Mao and his thugs seizing power in 1949. Delegates included East German SED Politburo member Egon Krenz, East German SED Central Committee member Wolfgang Rauchfuss, Miroslav Zavadil of the Central Committee of the Czechoslovak Communist Party and Chairman of the Central Council of Trade Unions of Czechoslovakia; pro-Chinese Vietnamese Communist in exile Hoang Van Hoan, Deputy Chairman of the Soviet-Chinese Friendship Society I.V. Arkhipov, Lionel Soto of the Central Committee of the Cuban Communist Party, Stefan Murin, Chairman of the Czechoslovakia-China Friendship Committee, Yi Cha-pang, Chairman of the State Commission of Science and Technology and chairman of the Korea-China Friendship Association from North Korea, North Korean Minister of Finance Yun Ki-chong, Mongolian Minister of Communications Binbzhav Batar, former Reagan era Secretary of State and Kissinger-globalist clone Alexander Haig, Ryoichi Kawai, President of the Japan-China Association on Economy and Trade, Takashi Mukaibo, Chairman of the Japan-China Society, Sir Adrian Swire, Chairman of Britain's Swire Group, and W. Dekker, President of Dutch Philips Company.[345]

---

[342] "National Day Parade in Peking" <u>Xinhua</u> October 2, 1984

[343] "Message from foreign countries" <u>Xinhua</u> October 2, 1984

[344] "Greetings on China's National Day" <u>BBC Summary of World Broadcasts</u> October 2, 1984,

[345] "Deng Ziaoping Meets Foreign Diplomats and Guests" <u>Xinhua</u> October 3, 1989

In August 1978, receptions which celebrated the creation of the Chinese People's Liberation Army took place in the Third World fascist or communist nations such as communist North Korea, socialist Burma, communist Laos, the Shah's Iran, communist Afghanistan, Mobutu's Zaire, socialist Zambia, socialist Mali, the communist Congo People's Republic, communist Mozambique, General Eyadema's Togo, militarist Argentina, communist East Germany, communist Hungary, and communist Czechoslovakia.[346]

By the late 1980s, open military relations were reportedly renewed between Soviet bloc countries and China. In October 1988, the Chinese Defense Minister Qin Jiwei reported that the exchange between senior Chinese and Hungarian military leaders *"signifies a new phase in the relations between the two countries' armed forces."* During the meeting with Hungarian Deputy Minister of Defense Jozsef, General Qin Jiwei, also a State Councilor, said *"relations between armed forces of China and Hungary have expanded rapidly in recent years. This is not only in the fundamental interests of the two peoples, but also conducive to world peace."* Lt-Gen Pacsek of the Hungarian People's Army expressed the hope for co-operation in military education, training and industry to his Chinese counterparts.[347]

In early November 1989, Zhou Peiyuan, Vice-Chairman of the CPPCC National Committee met with a delegation led by Bedrich Svestika, President of the Czechoslovak Peace Council.[348] In November 1989, a Chinese military delegation headed by Xu Xin, Deputy Chief of General Staff of the People's Liberation Army visited Prague and conferred with Czech Communist General Secretary Gustav Husak, Czechoslovak Defense Minister General Milan Vaclavih, and Army Chief of General Staff Colonel General Miroslav Vacek. Husak stated to Xu Xin that Czechoslovakia supported China's *"safeguarding socialism and maintaining world peace."* Husak added further that Czechoslovakia *"cherishes its relations with China and hopes to further overall cooperation with China."*[349]

Throughout the so-called *"split"* period, Romania and China maintained close military and intelligence relations. Perhaps when the *"split"* was first formulated, the *"independent"* Romanians were tasked by Moscow to retain close ties with an *"anti-Soviet"* China. If this hypothesis is true, then Moscow, Beijing, and Bucharest developed the perfect scenario of plausible denial of a strategic deception that was aimed against American policy makers. After all, Western and American policymakers who accepted the bona fides of Romanian *"independence"* from Moscow would certainly not be suspicious over the open connections between Beijing and Bucharest. During the reign of Chinese communist dictator Hua Guo-feng, Chinese intelligence passed on samples of film acquired from Kodak to their Romanian foreign intelligence (DIE) comrades. This film was sold to foreign tourists who visited Romania and exported abroad to earn American dollars for Romanian coffers.[350] In 1984, Romanian Defense Minister Constantin Olteanu and General Vasile Milea met with Chinese PLA General Yang

[346] "China's Army Day Anniversary Celebrated Abroad" Xinhua August 3, 1978
[347] "Defence Minister on 'new phase' in relations with Hungarian Army" Xinhua News Agency November 10, 1988
[348] "Czechoslovak peace delegation in China" Xinhua November 3, 1989
[349] "Czechoslovak Top Leaders Meet PLA Senior Officer" Xinhua General Overseas News Service November 2, 1989
[350] Pacepa. Ion. Red Horizons (Regnery Washington DC 1990) page 372.

Dezhi and extolled *"the friendly relations between the two peoples and armies."*[351] In September 1989, Romanian Defense Minister Vasile Milea noted that *"the Chinese People's Liberation Army (PLA) has proved with its actions to be an army loyal to socialism and the Chinese Communist Party."* Minister Milea met with General Guo Linxiang, Deputy Director of the General Political Department of the PLA and they noted *"the two sides highly appraised the relations of friendship and cooperation between the two armies, two parties and two peoples. They pledged continued efforts for further development of these relations."*[352]

The Chinese also healed their split with Yugoslavia in the 1970s and reopened close military and intelligence relations. In 1978, the Chinese intelligence agencies revamped their regional base in Belgrade under Wang Chenxi. In the early 1980s, Qiao Shi and Tao Siju travelled to Belgrade to enhance cooperation with Yugoslav intelligence (UDBA). When they arrived in Belgrade, Stane Dolanc, security chief for President Josip Broz Tito was asked to forge permanent intelligence ties with the Chinese. Those links have remained strong ever since, thanks partly to the efforts of Col. Slavko Milojevic, a one-time Yugoslav military attaché in Beijing. This relationship continued throughout the rule of the communist (LCY) and Milosevic (SPS-Socialist Party of Serbia) dictatorships.[353]

Chinese relations with North Korea continued to be very close. In February 1978, a declassified communist Romanian document noted that Red China granted North Korea a loan of $100 million in order to help repay Pyongyang's debt to Western banks.[354] In May 1981, a Chinese People's Liberation army delegation visited North Korea. The Chinese delegation was led by Deputy Chief of the General Staff Wu Xiuquan, Deputy CGS of the PLA and Deputy Commander of the Chinese Air Force Cao Lihuai. They met with Vice Minister of the People's Armed Forces of North Korea Lt-Gen Pak Chung-kuk and Lt-Gen Yun Chi-ho, Deputy Director of the General Political Bureau of the People's Armed Forces of Korea. Wu Xiuquan stated that *"The peoples and armies of China and Korea have sealed a solid friendship in blood in the protracted struggle against imperialism. We will closely co-operate, unite and march together with the Korean people and comrades-in-arms of the People's Army in the future cause of socialist construction."*[355] In May 1988 North Korean General O Chin-u met with *"Chinese comrades"* noting that this relationship between the two communist countries is characterized by: *"a special emotion that can be felt only between class brothers and comrades in arms."*[356] In April 1990, the Chinese Navy Admiral Li Yaowen paid a visit to North Korea. They were received by North Korean dictator Kim Il-sung, who praised the Chinese PLA for quelling *"the*

[351] "Chinese, Romanian Military Leaders Meet" The Xinhua General Overseas News Service July 14, 1984
[352] "Chinese Army Group Ends Visit to Romania" The Xinhua General Overseas News Service September 15, 1989
[353] "Chinese Agencies Lose a Friend" Intelligence Newsletter November 12, 1998
[354] Telegram 066.569 From the Romanian Embassy in Pyongyang to the Romanian Ministry of Foreign Affairs February 28, 1978 Accessed From: http://digitalarchive.org/document/116417
[355] "PLA Goodwill Delegation to N Korea" New China News Agency May 14, 1981
[356] "Speeches by DPRK Armed Forces Minister and Chinese Counterpart" Pyongyang Home Service May 21, 1988

anti-revolutionary riot last year and achieved national stability, unity and a success in economic construction."[357]

Even during the *"split,"* the Soviets surprisingly maintained a level of military relations with the Chinese PLA. In 1977, the Soviet military attaché in China Colonel V.I. Soloviev, hosted a reception in Beijing to commemorate the founding of the Soviet Army. Chinese visitors included the Deputy Chief of General Staff of the Chinese People's Liberation Army Wu Hsiu-Chuan, Deputy Commander of the PLA Garrison Li Chung-Chi, Deputy Director of the Foreign Affairs Bureau of the Ministry of National Defense Chang Ping-Yu, Deputy Director of the Department of Soviet Union and East European Affairs of the Foreign Ministry Ma Hsu-Sheng, Deputy Departmental Director of the Foreign Trade Ministry Li Shu-Chien, and the Permanent Director of the Chinese People's Association for Friendship with Foreign Countries Chung Han-Chiu.[358] Even more incredible was George Lardner's report that China had *"a significant military relationship"* with the Soviets even before Gorbachev took over the USSR. Furthermore, even the US Arms Control and Disarmament Agency reported that China purchased $310 million of weapons from the Soviet Union in the period from 1982 to 1986.[359] Perhaps it was these facts that convinced the defecting GRU Colonel Stanislav Lunev to report in a 1998 interview with J.R. Nyquist that he suspected that China and the USSR maintained a secret alliance during the 1980s. Lunev's assertion was based on observations while he was posted in Red China.[360]

Meanwhile, the Soviets continued to increase their trade ties with Beijing. In 1979, Deng Xiaoping stated to American industrialist and Soviet agent of influence Armand Hammer at a barbeque with Texas oilmen that *"No introduction is necessary for Dr. Hammer. We know him in China as the American who helped Lenin. Why don't you come to China and help us as well?"* In 1980, the Chinese bought 50,000 tons of Soviet urea through Occidental. Hammer noted *"The Chinese knew it was coming from Russia, so I think that bodes well for the future."*[361] In March 1982, three Chinese experts visited Moscow to study Soviet management techniques and were received by the deputy chairman of the Soviet State Planning Committee.[362] The Bank of China was a lead participant in the disbursement of a loan of $50 million for the Soviet Narodny Bank in November 1984.[363]

The Beijing International Trade Fair of July 1989 hosted delegations from South Korea, communist Hungary, the Soviet Union, communist Poland, communist Mongolia, pro-Soviet India, Thailand, and Islamist Iran. Single business delegations maintained booths from the United States (Advanced Medical Products Trading Corporation), Canada, Britain, West

[357] "Kim Il Sung Receives Chinese PLA Delegation" The Xinhua General Overseas News Service April 23, 1990
[358] "Soviet Military Attache in Peking Gives Reception to Mark Soviet Army Day" Xinhua February 24, 1977
[359] Lardner Jr., George and Smith, Jeffrey. "Intelligence Ties Endure Despite U.S.-China Strain; 'Investment' Is Substantial, Longstanding" The Washington Post June 25, 1989 page A1.
[360] Nyquist, Jeff. "Boycott China Anyway" WorldNetDaily April 16, 2001 Accessed http://www.wnd.com/index.php?pageId=8857
[361] Finder, Joseph. Red Carpet (Holt, Rinehart, and Winston, 1983) page 310.
[362] Golitsyn, Anatoli. New Lies for Old (Clarion House: Atlanta GA 1984) Accessed From: http://www.spiritoftruth.org/newlies4old.pdf
[363] Greenspon, Edward. "Hungarian bank raises eyebrows in U.K." The Globe and Mail (Canada) July 8, 1985

Germany, France, Italy, Japan, and Singapore at the Fair. Government trade bodies such as the Canada-China Trade Council, Korea Trade Promotion Corporation, West Germany's Ministry of Economics, the Italian Institute for Foreign Trade, and the Japan External Trade Organization also manned displays at the Fair. Nine South Korean companies displayed computers, televisions, vehicles, audio systems, textiles, and a piano at the Fair. The President of the China International Exhibition Center noted that the Fair was *an important venue for foreign business people.*[364]

The declassified minutes of the Central Committee Secretariat of the CPSU in 1990 revealed that cooperation existed between the Council on Mutual Economic Assistance (COMECON) and the Chinese Communist Party, the Korean Workers' Party (North Korea), the People's Revolutionary Party of Kampuchea (the Vietnamese puppet state in Cambodia), and the Lao People's Revolutionary Party (Laos).[365]

The Soviets continued to support the legitimacy of a Chinese conquest of Taiwan. In 1982, the Soviets expressed support for the One-China concept as proposed by Beijing. A Soviet radio broadcast expressed that *"the imperialists tried to create a situation of two Chinas."*[366] In late 1986, the Soviets stopped the jamming of Chinese radio broadcasts. Six years earlier, the CCP ceased jamming Soviet radio broadcasts to China.[367]

It was also clear that the USSR exported dual-use technologies to Red China, which more than likely provided tangible benefits for the weapons programs of the People's Liberation Army. In 1985, the Soviets and Chinese signed a contract for the purchase of 17 Tu-154M jet airliners.[368] In that same year, China also acquired Mi-8 helicopters ostensibly for *"disaster relief."*[369] The Soviets proposed in 1986 to export nuclear power plants to China.[370]

It even appeared that the Soviet and Chinese authorities collaborated in repatriating defectors who sought freedom in the West from communist tyranny. In August 1990, the Soviets forcibly repatriated a defecting Chinese pilot Senior Lt. Van Baoshi, who flew his MIG-19 jet fighter to Vladivostok and announced that he wanted to go to the United States. Baoshi was picked up by a Chinese civil aviation aircraft and transported back to the PRC, to a fate consisting of certain imprisonment or execution for defection.[371] In September 1991, several

[364] Fletcher, Noel. "Big Trade Fair in Beijing Opens on Muted Note" Journal of Commerce July 17, 1989 page 1A.
[365] Guide to the Archives of the Soviet communist party and Soviet state microfilm collection, 1903-1922: Russian State Archive of Contemporary History (Rossiiskii gosudarstvennyi arkhiv noveishei istorii - RGANI) Processed by Lora Soroka Hoover Institution Archives Stanford University Stanford, California 94305-6010 Accessed From: http://cdn.calisphere.org/data/13030/1z/kt767nf11z/files/kt767nf11z.pdf
[366] "USSR's Consistent Support for One China" Radio Peace and Progress May 28, 1982
[367] "USSR Said to Have Stopped Jamming of Russian Broadcasts From China" BBC Summary of World Broadcasts November 6, 1986
[368] "Purchase of Aircraft From the USSR" Xinhua July 22, 1985
[369] "China Imports Soviet Helicopters" BBC Summary of World Broadcasts May 28, 1985
[370] "USSR Reportedly Proposes Nuclear Facilities Exports to China" BBC Summary of World Broadcasts August 11, 1986
[371] "Soviets Extradite Chinese Pilot Who Wanted to Defect to U.S." Associated Press August 29, 1990

thousand Soviet KGB officers mysteriously *"fled"* to the PRC.[372] One could reasonably suggest that it was possible that these KGB officers were dispatched to China as part of an aid program to Beijing. In order to fool the United States, a cover story could have been developed about these KGB officers *"fleeing"* the USSR, despite the strict border controls of both the Soviet and Chinese governments. These governments generally do not allow people free access in and out of their nations. Hence, the claims that these KGB officers *"fled"* from the USSR to China was quite possibly specious at best.

By the end of the late 1980s, the Soviet-Chinese military relationship experienced an expansion of direct contacts. The Chinese delegation to the Farnborough Air Show (1988) in Great Britain remarked that Beijing intended to purchase Soviet-made missiles. In March 1989, the Kamov Design Bureau participated in an air show in Red China. Beijing invited Soviet specialists to visit a Chinese aircraft engine factory to determine the extent of assistance to be provided by Moscow. In November 1989, Chinese Foreign and Defense Ministry officials visited the USSR and discussed *"strengthening mutual trust and other issues."*[373] Red Chinese diplomats in Washington DC themselves reported that Soviet representatives were among the only guests at a 1989 Chinese Embassy reception which honored the People's Liberation Army.[374]

In April 1990, a delegation led by Chinese PLA General Song Wenzhong visited various Soviet military installations. Song met with Col. Gen. Mikhail Moiseyev, Chief of the Soviet General Staff. Moiseyev also met with Xu Xin, Deputy Chief of Staff of the Chinese PLA. In June 1990, Col. Gen. Liu Huaqing, Vice Chairman of the Central Military Commission met with Defense Minister General Dmitry Yazov, General Moiseyev, and Air Force General A.N. Yefimov.[375] In July 1990, General Xu Xin of the PLA met with Soviet veterans' groups.[376] In September and October of 1990, the Chinese and Soviets negotiated the purchase of Su-24 and Su-27 combat jet planes for Beijing's Air Force. In January 1991, the Soviets also signed a technical cooperation agreement for the provisioning of turbojet engine blades, titanium alloys, and advanced composite materials for the Chinese armed forces.[377] In May 1991, Soviet Defense Minister General Yazov concluded an agreement with China for a sale of 24 SU-27 jet fighter bombers to Beijing. China was also to acquire the technology and equipment from the USSR to produce these planes within the People's Republic[378] China also concluded a barter agreement with the USSR where they would take delivery of Soviet MIG-27 jet fighters in exchange for $733 million worth of food, consumer goods, and textiles that were manufactured by the PRC.[379]

[372] "KGB Agents Seek Early Retirement in China" The Independent September 5, 1991 page 1.
[373] "Military and Foreign Affairs Delegation to USSR" Xinhua November 15, 1989
[374] "Tracking Moscow's Activity Around the Globe" National Security Record September 8, 1989 page 1.
[375] Twining, David Thomas. Beyond Glasnost: Soviet Reform and Security Issues (Greenwood Publishing Group, 1992) pages 135-136.
[376] "General Xu Xin Meets Soviet Veterans" The Xinhua General Overseas News Service JULY 24, 1990
[377] Twining, David Thomas. Beyond Glasnost: Soviet Reform and Security Issues (Greenwood Publishing Group, 1992) page136.
[378] "China to Purchase 24 Soviet Fighter Jets" Japan Economic Journal May 25, 1991 page 14.
[379] Parker, Jeffrey K. "China's Price for Aid to Moscow: Cheap Fighters" United Press International March 14, 1991

In August 1991, General Chi Haotian of the PLA visited the USSR and met with Soviet Defense Minister Dmitry Yazov. Xinhua noted *"the two men said they believed the contact between Chinese and Soviet people and the two armies would continually strengthen and develop. During his one-week official and friendly visit to the Soviet Union, Chi also held a departing talk with Mikhail Moiseev, Chief of the General Staff of the Soviet Armed Forces. While staying in the Soviet Union, the Chinese guests visited Moscow, Volgograd, Sevastopol, Kiev and Leningrad. They also met with leaders in the military districts of North Caucasia, Kiev and Leningrad and the Black Sea Fleet, and visited military facilities and observed strategic manoeuvres there."*[380] In July 1991, General Xu Xin, Deputy Chief of the General Staff of the PLA met with Soviet veterans' groups.[381] In June 1991, PLA Chief of General Staff Gen. Chi Haotian met with Senior General VM Arhipov, Soviet Deputy Minister of Defense and Chief of the Main Board of Army in the Rear. Chi noted that the visit *"would contribute to the development of the existing friendly relations between the two nations and armies."* Arhipov noted *"that the PLA has become strong armed forces, and he was satisfied with the growth of the friendly ties between the two armies. Both sides expressed willingness to further enhance the friendship between the two armies."* Xinhua also noted that General Zhao Nanqi, member of the Central Military Commission and Director of the General Logistics Department of the PLA met with Arhipov.[382]

China's trade, intelligence, and military relations with the other Eastern European communist countries was also both quantitatively and qualitatively expanded. China's Ministry of State Security (MSS) and the East German Stasi collaborated with each other before the fall of the Berlin Wall in late 1989. Ceausescu's Securitate also maintained close relations with the Chinese intelligence and security apparatus.[383] In 1980, an American official who was present in a delegation that visited Red China reported that Beijing was *"already buying computers from Romania, but the memory core is very limited."*[384] The Chinese F-7 fighter jet was powered by a Soviet designed MIG-21 engine that Beijing received from Warsaw Pact member Romania.[385] It is possible that Moscow delegated to Romania the task of supplying select types of militarily relevant Soviet technology to Bucharest during the Sino-Soviet *"split"* period. Yugoslavia received a Chinese order for two 45,000 DWT tankers in 1976. In November 1976 the Chinese completed the Valias Coal Dressing Plant in Albania. In 1978, Yugoslav Vice-Premier Berislav

---

[380] "Chinese Military Leader Ends USSR Visit" Xinhua General Overseas News Service August 12, 1991

[381] "PLA General Staff Deputy Chief Meets Soviet Visitors" The Xinhua General Overseas News Service July 10, 1991

[382] "Chinese Army Chief Meets Soviet Deputy Defence Minister" The Xinhua General Overseas News Service June 21, 1991

[383] "The Chinese Secret Service: From Mao to the Olympic Games" Intellibriefs March 14, 2008 Accessed: http://intellibriefs.blogspot.com/2008/03/chinese-secret-service-from-mao-to.html

[384] Robinson, Jr., Clarence A. "China's Technology Impresses Visitors" Aviation Week & Space Technology October 6, 1980 page 25.

[385] Cooley, John K. "Western 'dual technology' may be on its way to China" Christian Science Monitor July 10, 1980 page 10.

Sefer concluded a trade agreement with China for $300 million per year worth of imports of Chinese oil and coal.[386]

Throughout the 1980s, the Red Chinese also lent ideological and material support to anti-American causes. In 1983, China declared its support for *"national liberation movements in southern Africa and the people of Central America, and condemned the United States for invading Grenada. The CCP has also helped promote Arab unity and given form support to the Palestinian people."*[387] In 1982, New China News Agency correspondent Chen Weibin noted that *"The peace movement is growing vigorously in the West partly because the economic situation in the United States and Western Europe has deteriorated since the end of last year. These countries are suffering from growing financial deficits, worsening inflation, and rising unemployment, but the governments of these Western countries keep increasing military spending. This has led the people in these countries to demand budget cuts for military expenditures, a cessation of the nuclear arms race, more social welfare, and an increase in job opportunities."*[388] Deng Liqun of the CCP Central Committee noted that *"the CCP fully understands, respects, and supports the anti-nuclear movement in West Europe, Japan, and the United States."*[389] CCP General Secretary Hu Yaobang noted that: *"Peace movements the world over are waving a tenacious struggle towards the end. Our 1 billion Chinese people are prepared to join hands with peace movements the world over in unremitting efforts for world peace."*[390]

Internal security expert Judge Robert Morris noted that *"...the two communist powers are resolving their differences. Both now support the MPLA regimes in Angola, SWAPO in Namibia, ZANU in Zimbabwe, the Shining Path in Peru, Castro in his adventures, the PLO, the ANC in South Africa, and the Puerto Rican terrorists."* The former American Ambassador to the UN and Democratic Senator Daniel Patrick Moynihan observed that China voted against the United States 86%, thus placing Beijing *"in the same column as the Soviet Union."*[391]

In another study, China was found to have voted against the United States' position over 70% of the time. The Red Chinese condemned the Camp David Accords, called for sanctions against South Africa, and supported a Cuban-initiated UN resolution which called for the greater economic rights and less human and political freedoms. In 1981, China also increased trade with Poland by thirty percent during the imposition of open martial law by General Jaruzelski.[392]

According to former US Air Force General Joseph Churba, the Chinese criticized the Strategic Defense Initiative (SDI) as an American attempt to *"militarize space."* Churba noted further that *"The Chinese had no response as to why they were more concerned about American*

---

[386] Woodard, Kim. The International Energy Relations of China (Stanford University Press, 1980) pages 69-70.
[387] "CCP Expands Contacts with Foreign Political Parties" Xinhua December 29, 1983.
[388] "Chinese View of the Western Peace Movement" Xinhua April 23, 1983
[389] "China's Support for European Peace Movement: Freedom for Writers" Xinhua October 13, 1983
[390] "CCP General Secretary on China's Opposition to Arms Races" Xinhua June 11, 1985
[391] Morris, Robert. Our Globe Under Siege III (J&W Enterprises: Mantoloking NJ 1988) page 27.
[392] "Despite FX Cancellation: Red China Undermines US Foreign Policy" Human Events March 6, 1982 page 186-187.

than about Soviet strategic defenses."[393] The Chinese Communists denounced President Reagan's proposal for Strategic Defense Initiative (SDI) in 1985. Deng Xiaoping stated that SDI would *"The 'Star Wars' plan must not be carried out because it would cause qualitative change in the arms race between the superpowers."*[394]

Instead of opposing the Soviet military buildup in North Korea during 1986, the Chinese instead condemned the presence of American military forces in South Korea as *"provocative."*[395]

Despite the supposedly friendly relations with the United States, Beijing sought to inflame anti-Americanism within the Chinese masses. An Iranian-style hostage crisis was planned by Beijing to hit back at limited American support for anti-communist dissidents. In June 1989, the Red Chinese planned to *"arouse the masses"* to surround the US Embassy in Beijing and then seize any American official coming out. The Chinese then planned to hold a US Embassy official hostage in exchange for the dissidents Fang Lizhi and Li Shuxian.[396]

Even the Maoist splinter parties were viewed as long term Soviet assets by some Western observers. James L. Tyson noted that *"The Soviets regularly go so far as to give secret support to Trotskyite or Maoist groups that are ostensibly opposed to the Soviet Union or supporting Communist China. The only criterion is that they be opposed to the United States on the principle that the enemy of my enemy is my friend."*[397]

Fred Schwarz noted that *"The CPML*[398] *has not renounced the ultimate fight with the West, but believes it will come after the victory over Russia. In preparation for the fight against capitalism, the CPML maintains it is necessary to have 'well selected communists working appropriately and biding their time' within Western society. Recently, there have been 'talks' between the CPML and the Communist Party of Australia. It is difficult to assess their significance. **Internationally, although Peking avows 'furious hatred' for Russia, it should never be forgotten that both are Marxist-Leninist countries. In this sense they are squabbling brothers. And blood brothers may suddenly unite in common cause**.*"[399]

China also shifted to supporting the communist MPLA in Angola during most of the 1980s. In 1979, the MPLA indicated interest in forging ties with the Chinese Communist Party.[400] The All-China Federation of Trade Unions issued this statement of support for the MPLA in 1982: *"The All-China Federation of Trade Unions has expressed firm support for the Angolan workers' just struggle. In a message to the National Union of Angolan Workers on 16th August the federation said that the Chinese workers and trade unions strongly condemn the South African troops large-scale invasion of Angola, firmly support the Angolan workers and*

---

[393] Churba, Joseph. The Washington Compromise (University Press of America 1995) pages 151-152.
[394] "China's Top Leader Criticizes Star Wars" Associated Press August 2, 1985
[395] Churba, Joseph. The Washington Compromise (University Press of America 1995) pages 151-152.
[396] "Reports of Chinese plans to take US hostage, Fang Lizhi's departure" BBC Summary of World Broadcasts June 16, 1989
[397] Tyson, James L. Target America (Regnery Gateway, 1985) page 26.
[398] The Communist Party of Australia (Marxist-Leninist)
[399] Schwarz Report October 15, 1983 Accessed From: http://www.schwarzreport.org/uploads/schwarz-report-pdf/schwarz-report-1983-10-15.pdf
[400] "Angolan Move Towards Establishing Relations with China" BBC Summary of World Broadcasts January 23, 1979

people in their just struggle to resist aggression and defend national territory, and resolutely support the Namibian workers and people in their just struggle for national liberation."[401]

In October 1988, the CCP and the MPLA signed cooperation accords covering the fields of economy, technology, and trade.[402] In January 1988, Jiang Guanghua of the CCP International Liaison Department visited Angola and conferred with Foreign Minister Alfonso Dunem Nbinda and the Secretary General of the Angolan National Union of Workers.[403]

Even into the Deng era, the Chinese continued to maintain relations with various Palestinian terrorist groups. In 1980, a delegation of PLO Fatah officials visited the People's Republic and met with Chinese Foreign Minister Huang Hua. Minister Huang and Abu Jihad of the PLO Fatah proclaimed their continued friendship and denounced Israel.[404] In September 1980, the PLO reportedly signed military agreements with China, North Korea, and the Islamic Fascist state in Pakistan. These three states pledged to supply weapons and train PLO cadres.[405] Yasir Arafat visited China in 1984 and toured tank units of the PLA. He met with Chinese premier Zhao Ziyang, who promised that *"China would provide the cause of Palestinian liberation with political, material and moral assistance within its capability..."*[406] In 1989, the PLO Political Department Head Faruq Qaddumi met with Chinese Prime Minister Li Peng, who pledged Beijing's continued anti-Israel policy: *"The Chinese people have always supported the Palestinian people's struggle against Israeli aggression and expansion. We did so in the past and we will continue to do so in the future. Our principled position will remain unchanged unless Israel gives up its policy of aggression and expansion."*[407] These supportive words were translated into concrete action through the provisioning of the PLO with weapons (artillery and ammunition) and military training. The United States was denounced by the Red Chinese for their support for the State of Israel.[408]

China also supported battle of the Southwest Africa People's Organization (SWAPO) to create a communist Namibia. A SWAPO delegation led by Sam Nujoma met with Chinese Premier Zhao Ziyang, who stated in 1983 that: *"We have not only supported you politically and morally, but also provided as much material assistance as we can. No matter what changes in the world situation, China will remain firm in supporting your just cause."*[409] The Azanian People's Liberation Army (APLA) was formed as Poqo in 1961. Its headquarters were located in Tanzania and its front line terrorists fought to create a South Africa governed under the precepts of Maoist Communism and racial collectivism. APLA/Poqo soldiers were trained in Libya, Egypt, Red China and Yugoslavia.[410] In August 1988, Mozambican Defense Minister Alberto

---

[401] "PRC Trade Unions Support Angola" New China News Agency August 26, 1982

[402] "China and Angola Sign Cooperation Agreements" Xinhua October 24, 1988

[403] "Chinese CP Delegation in Angola Meeting with Mbinda" Luanda Home Service January 13, 1988

[404] "Fatah Delegation's Visit to China and N Korea" New China News Agency August 28, 1980

[405] "In Brief: General Outcome of Abu Jihad's Far East visit" Israel home service September 9, 1980

[406] "Yasir Arafat's Visit to China" Xinhua May 8, 1984

[407] "PLO Official in China Talks With Li Peng and Zhao Ziyang" Peking Home Service February 17, 1989

[408] "China Boosts Aid to PLO, Denounces U.S." The Associated Press December 4, 1983

[409] "SWAPO Delegation in China: Military Aid" Xinhua February 2, 1983

[410] "Pan-Africanist Congress's armed wing to disband formally" SAPA March 18, 1999

Chipande noted *"that the PRC and the DPRK[411] are interested in supporting the reorganization process of the Mozambican armed forces…Mozambican military delegations will visit the two countries soon to identify possible areas of co-operation."[412]*

The Chinese and North Koreans were also reported to have attempted to ship firearms in 1987 to the communist New People's Army fighting against the governments of Marcos and Aquino.[413]

In 1977, it was reported that China was providing rifles to the Ethiopian military of the communist junta called the Dergue.[414] The Arms Control and Disarmament Agency (ACDA) estimated that Red China sent $20 million worth of arms to Ethiopia.[415] The General Secretary of the Chinese Communist Party Zhao Ziyang and Ethiopian ruler Mengistu signed a cooperation agreement in June 1988.[416] In a meeting with Chinese ruler Deng Xiaoping, Ethiopian dictator Mengistu stated in 1988 that *"Ethiopia is China's sincere friend and he wished China's socialist construction success."[417]* In December 1988, Mengistu and the high level Chinese Communist Party official Yang Rudai met to discuss cooperation. Rudai noted that the talks focused *"on the implementation of these objectives in various spheres and on the promotion of co-operation."* Rudai also observed that *"the talks between the two parties would strengthen mutual co-operation, achievements and bilateral relations. He added that the WPE could gain by sharing the experiences of the veteran CCP."[418]* In July 1989, Workers Party of Ethiopia Politburo member Shimelis Mazengia stated to Chinese Communist Central Committee Secretary Jiang Zemin that *"We are glad to see that China has brought the situation under control."* He was of course referring to the Chinese PLA repression of the student demonstrators in Tiananmen Square.[419] In October 1990, a Workers Party of Ethiopia delegation led by Politburo member Shimelis Mazengia visited North Korea and Red China to consolidate their alliances.[420] In January 1991, the government-controlled trade unions of Ethiopia and Red China exchanged views on mutual cooperation and the workers' movements in Africa and the world.[421]

North Korea also received some Type 59 tanks from Red China in 1982 and 1983. In 1983, China sold 260 Type 69 tanks to Baathist Iraq. By the 1980s, countries such as Somalia,

---

[411] Democratic People's Republic of Korea, also known as North Korea.

[412] "Mozambique Defence Minister on co-operation with China and North Korea" Maputo home service August 23, 1988

[413] Del Mundo, Fernando. "Government thwarts rebels arms deal with China, North Korea" United Press International November 12, 1987

[414] Ottaway, David B. "Ethiopian Military Relies on Peasants for Its Defense" Washington Post March 22, 1977 page A14.

[415] Cordesman, Anthony H. The Military Balance and Arms Sales in Yemen and the Red Sea States: 1986-1992 Center for Strategic and International Studies September, 1993 Accessed From: http://csis.org/files/media/csis/pubs/9309_yemen&redseamilbal.pdf

[416] "Ethiopian President in China" Xinhua June 25, 1988

[417] Ibid.

[418] "Ethiopia Chinese CP delegation ends visit" BBC Summary of World Broadcasts December 28, 1988

[419] "Chinese party leader receives Ethiopian party delegation" Xinhua July 19, 1989

[420] "Ethiopia Politburo member returns from North Korea and China" Voice of Ethiopia External Service October 26, 1990

[421] "Chinese trade unionists in Ethiopia" Xinhua News Agency February 5, 1991

Sudan, North Korea, Albania, Pakistan, Zaire, the Congo People's Republic, Mozambique, North Vietnam, Tanzania, and Zimbabwe received the same types of Chinese tanks.[422]

In December 1984, China dispatched resident military attachés to Cuba. Cuba also backed the Chinese government for their crackdown in Tiananmen Square in 1989. The Cuban foreign minister commended Chinese authorities for *"defeating the counterrevolutionary acts."*[423] In 1990, Gen. Chi Haotian, Chief of General Staff of the Chinese PLA, met with Lt-Gen Ulises Rosales, Chief of General Staff of the Cuban Revolutionary Armed Forces (FAR) in Beijing. The Xinhua release noted that *"Chi and Rosales expressed the hope that friendship and co-operation between China and Cuba and between their armed forces will continue to grow in the days to come."*[424]

The Chinese also hailed the closer North Korean-Soviet ties occurring in the 1980s. A PRC Foreign Ministry spokesman stated the Chinese *"positively appraise"* the North Korean's *"independent foreign policy and are pleased to see the development of its relations with the Soviet Union."*[425]

Former PRK[426] diplomat Chhin Sun-An said *"The national reconciliation policy of the Phnom Penh government did not come from the goodwill of Hanoi and Phnom Penh. It was the result of Soviet pressure…Soviet Deputy Foreign Minister Kapitsa once told the Phnom Penh government that it should talk with the Khmer Rouge so that the USSR could reduce Chinese-Soviet tension and isolate the USA."*[427]

By the end of 1989 and 1990, the Chinese also improved relations with the Vietnamese puppet communist regimes in Laos and Cambodia. As of September 1989, the chief editor of a PRK government-sponsored magazine in Phnom Penh reported that three Red Chinese officials discussed the resumption of trade ties with communist Cambodian regime. These Chinese officials were part of a Thai business group. It was reported by an Eastern European diplomat that PRK military officers met with Chinese officials in Laos.[428] In September 1990, the Chinese and Vietnamese Communist leaders held a secret summit in Chengdu, China. Reportedly, China offered to replace the entire Soviet aid program to Vietnam with one of its own in return for Vietnam's agreement to *"co-ordinate"* its foreign policy and develop closer political ties with China.[429] Red China even served as an intermediary for busting the American *"embargo"* on Vietnamese products. As of January 1990, Vietnam utilized a circuitous route to export its

---

[422] Gilks, Anne and Segal, Gerald. <u>China and the Arms Trade</u> (Croom Helm, 1985) pages 66-69.

[423] Minson Adam and Erikson, Daniel P. "Cuba and China" Accessed From: http://www.hemisferio.org/documentos/cuba.and.china.pdf

[424] "Chinese Army Chief Meets Cuban Military Delegation" <u>Xinhua</u> April 30, 1990

[425] Southerland, Daniel "China Lauds N. Korea for its Soviet Ties" <u>Washington Post</u> September 12, 1985 page A25.

[426] PRK was the acronym of the Vietnamese puppet communist regime of the People's Republic of Kampuchea, which succeeded the communist Khmer Rouge dictatorship, which was officially known as Democratic Kampuchea.

[427] "Voice of the Khmer Interviews Defecting Phnom Penh Diplomat" <u>Voice of the Khmer</u> October 31, 1989

[428] "China Denies Contacts With Phnom Penh Government" <u>The Associated Press</u> September 28, 1989

[429] Thayer, Carlyle A. <u>The Vietnam People's Army Under Doi Moi</u> (Diane Publishing Company, 1994) page 68.

products to the capitalist world. Vietnam would sell its cashews in the shell to Hong Kong and then they were sold to Red China. They are processed in Red China and then sold abroad to countries like the United States. They are marked as *"Made in China."*[430]

Soviet satellites in the Third World also welcomed the rapprochement between Beijing and Moscow as a victory for the forces of world communism and a blow to imperialism. The Vietnamese communist newspaper <u>Nhan Dan</u> noted that this open Sino-Soviet rapprochement *"benefits not only the peoples of the USSR and China but also peace and security in the world. It also helps improve the atmosphere in Asia and the Pacific."* Such a development *"wins the sympathy from the public at large in various countries."*[431] In June 1989, the Yemen Socialist Party General Secretary and South Yemen ruler Salim al-Bid exulted that *"we in Democratic Yemen experience considerable happiness at the positive development of Sino-Soviet relations. We consider that the interests of the two big socialist countries and the interests of the other socialist states, as well as liberation and peace in the world, are best served by understanding and co-operation between those two countries..."*[432] In July 1990, Heng Samrin stated *"We welcome the improvement in relations between the Soviet Union and China and between China and Vietnam, relations that will greatly influence the international and regional policy as well as the political solution to the Cambodian problem..."*[433]

The Chinese also defended the hard-line elements in the Warsaw Pact against any manifestations of *"reformist"* socialism and alleged attempts by the West and the Americans to undermine communism. China expressed these concerns in 1989 by stating: *"The entire imperialist Western world is vainly attempting to make the socialist countries drop the socialist road and eventually bring them under the control of international monopoly capital. We must stand up to this tide and take a clear-cut stand."*[434]

Soviet allies in the Third World and the Warsaw Pact also supported or acted as apologists for the Chinese massacre of students in Tiananmen Square. In June 1989, the East German magazine <u>Young World</u> noted in reference to the massacre of students in Red China: *"See the handiwork of counter-revolutionaries who are endangering socialism in China."*[435] The Soviets refused to show scenes of the demonstrations in Tiananmen Square on their state television network in 1989. Gorbachev reportedly scolded the demonstrators as *"hotheads."* Specifically, the Soviet dictator stated to his Chinese allies: *"We, too, have hotheads who want to renovate socialism overnight. But it doesn't happen in real life. Only in fairy tales."* Soviet newspaper <u>Pravda</u> dismissively noted: *"It appears that in an attempt to exploit the current situation in order to put pressure on the government, the students have lost the support of many people who sympathized with them."* (This was written by their political commentator Vsevolod

[430] "Vietnam's Solution to Trade Barriers: 'Zigzag'" <u>Journal of Commerce</u> January 2, 1990 page 1A.
[431] "Nhan Dan Welcomes Normalisation of Sino-Soviet Relations" <u>Nhan Dan</u> May 22, 1989
[432] "PDRY Party Leader on Economic And Political Reform and Yemeni Unity" <u>Aden Home Service</u> June 27, 1989
[433] "Heng Samrin KPRP 'Remains Loyal to...Lenin" <u>Voice of the People of Cambodia</u> July 6, 1990
[434] "US-Red Chinese Ties Seen Unlikely to Improve Soon" <u>Central News Agency-Taiwan</u> August 27, 1989
[435] Bassett, Richard. "A sense of desperation grips Herr Honecker's Stalinist bastion; Gorbachov's visit to West Germany" <u>The Times (London)</u> June 13 1989

Ovchinnikov.)[436] Top secret files that were smuggled out by Pavel Stroilov indicated that Gorbachev openly supported the Chinese army's actions in Tiananmen Square in 1989: *"Thus, notes taken at Politburo meeting on 4 October 1989 read: Lukyanov reports that the real number of casualties in Tiananmen Square was 3,000.*
Gorbachev: *We must be realists. They, like us, have to defend themselves. Three thousand…So what?"*[437]

The Soviets and Chinese proudly displayed their desire for an alliance in their public statements as well. In a June 1991 meeting of CPSU and CCP delegations, General Secretary Jiang Zemin noted that to *"maintain friendly and good-neighbourly relations between China and the Soviet Union is in the interest of world peace and stability."*[438]

Top secret documents highlighted the admissions by Soviet bloc and Chinese Communist leaders to a mutual adherence to the common goal of the triumph of world communism and the defeat of the United States. A declassified transcript of a conversation between Bulgarian Communist dictator Todor Zhivkov and Chinese communist leaders Zhao Ziyang and Deng Xiaoping revealed that even alleged communist *"rivals"* still adhered to a common goal. This goal was undoubtedly world communism. Zhivkov travelled to Beijing for this high level meeting with Chinese leaders Deng Xiaoping and Zhao Ziyang. When the topic of Chinese Soviet relations came up, Zhao stated: *"As for China's relations with other countries, I suppose that our relations with the Soviet Union are of interest to you. We are pursuing a complete normalization of our relations with the Soviet Union. We would like the relations between the two great neighboring socialist countries to be normalized as soon as possible. The whole world would benefit from this."* Zhivkov agreed, noting that *"**I most sincerely hope that a way to normalize the relations between China and the Soviet Union will be found. We share common aims and ideals**."*[439]

In another meeting that year Zhivkov and Deng noted that a common ideological alliance had been solidified:
*"**TODOR ZHIVKOV**: Thus our attempts are directed at implementing the resolutions of the latest 13th Congress of our Party that was held last spring. **We will be together in our common struggle side by side**.*
***DENG XIAOPING**: **We share a common aim. We must make efforts together**.*
***TODOR ZHIVKOV**: Despite all that happened to the relations between our two socialist*

[436] Remnick, David "Moscow TV Shutters Glasnost in Coverage of Beijing Protests" Washington Post May 18, 1989 page A38
[437] Stroilov, Pavel "The Gorbachev Files" Spectator March 26, 2011 Accessed From: http://findarticles.com/p/articles/mi_qa3724/is_20110326/ai_n57158714/
[438] "Russian Party Delegation in China Discusses Ties and Socialism" Xinhua July 1, 1991
[439] "Meeting of Comrade Todor Zhivkov with Zhao Ziyang, Acting Secretary General of the Central Committee of the Chinese Communist Party and President of the State Council of China People's Republic Beijing", 6 May 1987 Accessed From Cold War International History Project Accessed From:
http://www.wilsoncenter.org/index.cfm?topic_id=1409&fuseaction=va2.document&identifier=5034BD72-96B6-175C-9BB8DC1F59FAEAB4&sort=Subject&item=Todor%20Zhivkov

countries, we are actually following the same path. This is what matters. All other problems can be solved by negotiating in a communist manner."[440]

Polish Foreign Minister Orzechowski noted in a secret document recounting his meeting with Chinese Foreign Minister Wu Xueqian in March 1987 that *"**While expressing his satisfaction with the development of relations between parties and nations, (Polish President Jaruzelski) stressed that one fundamental element which binds our countries is their political system and the common enemy**.*"[441]

In May 1987, Ceausescu highlighted his strong agreement with the open Sino-Soviet rapprochement and the coming unity of the entire communist world in a discussion with Soviet dictator Gorbachev. Ceausescu remarked that "*... In regard to the relationships between the Soviet Union and the other socialist countries and China, we salute this process of normalization, of improvement of relationships, and we deem it very important. We also salute the improvement of the relationships between the Soviet Union and China, and hope that a high-level meeting between them will take place in the long run. In fact, the Chinese comrades have declared that they are ready to go to Moscow. In my view, this is not difficult to arrange, and the possibility exists of some positive results being reached. Comrade Deng Xiaoping told me that although it was difficult for him to travel to Moscow, he was willing to do so.*
Comrade M. S. Gorbachev: *We must help (Deng Xiaoping), we can help him.*
Comrade Nicolae Ceausescu: *I am convinced that this can be done...This (agreement on Kampuchea and the Vietnamese presence) would have huge significance not only for the respective region but also for the relationships between the socialist countries, inclusively for the normalization of the relationships between the Soviet Union and China, for the general growth of the influence of socialist countries in the region. We take the view that we have to insist for (the adoption of) this solution.*"

At the same meeting, Ceausescu also argued for the furtherance of the broad unity of the world communist and leftist forces, thus overcoming any sectarian differences and uniting against the West. Ceausescu noted: "*Being Communists, being Communist parties, we bear the responsibility– not only to our peoples but also to the world Communist movement–of discussing and finding the ways of acting better in this field and in general, in the development of collaboration with the socialists, the social democrats, and other forces. We stand for a broad collaboration, a broad front of peace, but we think we cannot dissolve, so to say, the Communist movement in a front where the Communists do not exist any longer. On the contrary, the Communist movement should play an active role for the very fulfillment of the mission it has in uniting all of the forces and peoples. If our parties reached this conclusion, I would salute it...*"[442]

[440] "Talks with Zhao Ziyang and Deng Xiaoping in Beijing" May 7, 1987 Accessed from the Cold War International History Project Accessed From: http://wilsoncenter.org/index.cfm?topic_id=1409&fuseaction=va2.document&identifier=5034BD62-96B6-175C-9E795F8F67764934&sort=Collection&item=Bulgaria%20in%20the%20Cold%20War
[441] Informational Note From the Official Visit in Poland of the PRC Foreign Minister, Comrade Wu Xueqian (March 10-13, 1987) March 17, 1987 Accessed From: http://digitalarchive.wilsoncenter.org/document/113770
[442] "Speech of comrade Nicolae Ceausescu at the working meeting of the general secretaries and first secretaries of the Central Committees of the Communist and Workers' parties of the

Ceausescu also elaborated that *"We welcome the development of relations between the Soviet Union and the PRC, between the CPSU and the Communist Party of China. We consider this to be a very important event, and Romania has, as you know, has always insisted that this had to happen. We welcome this course."*[443]

The newspaper <u>Cheng Ming</u> reported in mid-1991 that Chinese dictator Deng Xiaoping called for the construction of a new axis of communist countries under the leadership of China and the Soviet Union. The Soviets were to train massive numbers of Chinese pilots, officers, and other military officers. Weapons previously stationed in the Warsaw Pact were to be withdrawn and transshipped to the developing axis of communist countries in Asia. The article's full text read as follows: *"'It is fortunate to see the USSR's party and people wake up...I think the USSR is redeemable, and I just do not believe that socialism with 70 years of history will collapse because of a few difficulties...This is a bitter lesson for communists in the whole world!...China and the USSR are neighbours. The CCP and the CPSU have traditional friendship and cooperative relations; when they have difficulties, we must give them our hand and help them. Of course, on a problem of basic principle, we must not give up our stand.'"*

Based on Deng's openly pro-Soviet positions in 1991, the Central Committee of the Chinese Communist Party called for a *"new socialist 'alliance circle' comprising the five nations of China, the USSR, North Korea, Mongolia and Vietnam."* Deng's strategy also utilized the strategy of deception/strategic retreats in order not to overly antagonize the West and the United States and jeopardize trade and technology transfers and privileges: *"When facing the West, do not struggle over some trivial problems, but make appropriate concessions so as to win economic aid from the West; in particular, utilize Japan's economic strength."*

The Soviet Defense Minister also agreed to provide the Red Chinese with heavy weapons that were previously stationed in Eastern Europe. The Soviets agreed to sell to China these weapons for very low prices, *"even at the price of 'scrap iron,' if China will pay the transport fees."* The Central Committee of the Chinese Communist Party was interested in the specifics of this deal. Chinese pilots, artillery troops, armored troops, and paratroops were also to be dispatched to Soviet military academies for training.[444]

By 1991, relations between the Soviet Union and China reached the level of the 1950s. The newspaper <u>Cheng Ming</u> reported that: *"the CCP began to give publicity to Sino-Soviet friendship, praising the USSR's fraternal assistance to China in the past, and propagating the 'great achievements' of the October Revolution. Large numbers of Soviet feature films have been shown. Over 20 kinds of Soviet reading materials have been reprinted, published and distributed among troops..."* Soviet aid also apparently played a role in Red China's future war plans against its long range enemies of Taiwan, Japan, and the United States: *"It has been revealed that the Central Military Commission of the CCP Central Committee has decided to strengthen the*

states participating in the Warsaw Treaty" 29 May 1987 Accessed From: ftp://budgie3.ethz.ch/php/documents/collection_14/05291987_2.htm

[443] Speech by the General Secretary of the Romanian Communist Party and President of the Socialist Republic of Romania, Comrade Nicolae Ceausescu at the Meeting of the PCC of the Warsaw Treaty Member-States Bucharest, 7-8 July 1989 Accessed From: http://www.php.isn.ethz.ch/collections/colltopic.cfm?lng=en&id=19041&navinfo=14465

[444] "Deng Xiaoping's Remarks on Relations With the USA and USSR and DPRK" <u>Cheng Ming</u> June 6, 1991

building of China's air force to make preparations for future wars. It is one of the major tasks in the building of the air force to send pilots to the USSR for further study... "[445]

The high level Chinese Communist Yang Shangkun called a meeting of the General Logistics Department, the PLA General Staff, and concerned State Council units in October 1991. He allegedly instructed them on how to further achieve China's consolidation of its relations with anti-US states and using this alliance as a means of conducting a hostile policy against the Americans. It was admitted once again that the purpose of the Sino-Soviet alliance was to strategically checkmate the United States. Arms exports to friendly Third World countries were also viewed by the CCP as a tool to further consolidate an anti-US alliance under Beijing's leadership. Yang reportedly stated: *"that the CCP has continued to export arms after the Gulf war. Because of the Most-Favoured-Nation status problem, it has not been doing it overtly and openly but on the sly. The CCP thought it could use the Soviet Union as a chip by striking a pose of Sino-Soviet alliance in bargaining with the USA. A high-ranking official from the General Logistics Department revealed the CCP remains firm in exporting arms because it wants to counteract the USA and hostile Western forces. Obviously China's insistence on exporting arms to Pakistan, Iraq and other countries is aimed at opposing US power politics, apart from earning foreign exchange. This high-ranking official said 'Iran and Iraq enjoy outstanding status in the Middle East. Though Iraq has been defeated, China believes that in a few years' time it will come back. Iraq's Husayn will absolutely not bow his head. Our support for Iraq is our attempt to build anti-US bases in the Middle East.'"* [446]

Meanwhile, some brave politicians, commentators, scholars, military officers, and intelligence officials attempted to sound the alarm over the threat of an emerging Sino-Soviet axis and Beijing's consistent anti-American foreign policies. Republican Presidential Candidate Ronald Reagan noted in an interview that: *"They (USSR and China) were allies and the only argument that caused their split was an argument over how to best destroy us."* Reagan was then asked if elected, would his administration support the sale of weapons to Communist China: *"No, because...they could turn right around and the day after tomorrow discover that they and the Soviets have more in common than they have with us."* [447] Unfortunately, President Reagan reneged on the spirit of his earlier concerns from the campaign of 1980 and continued the Nixon-Ford-Kissinger-Carter policy of appeasing the Chinese communists through trade concessions and technology exports.

Republican Congressman Phil Crane (R-IL) observed in reference to President Reagan's 1984 trip to China: *"I think the purpose was press coverage. It's interesting that when China censored the President's speeches, it censored the things he said about Russia. This shows with whom the Red Chinese are really in bed."* [448] In an article dated from 1986, former CIA Deputy Director Ray Cline noted that *"The PRC has opposed almost every American foreign policy position adopted since he (Deng) came to power."* [449] Dr. Ku Cheng Kang of the World Anti-Communist League noted that: *"The Soviet Union and Red China are attempting to form a new*

[445] Ni, Tso. "Hong Kong Paper on Sino-Soviet Relations; USSR to Train Chinese Pilots" <u>Cheng Ming</u> May 3, 1991
[446] "Cheng Ming on Deng Xiaoping's Inspection of New Fighter Plane; Arms Exports" <u>Cheng Ming</u> October 4, 1991
[447] Pelton, Robert W. <u>Traitors and Treason</u> (Lightning Source Incorporated, 2002) page 14.
[448] "Scoreboard" <u>American Opinion</u> July-August 1984 page 37.
[449] Cline, Ray S. "China's Conversion is Cause for Caution" <u>World and I</u> Issue1/1986 page 95

united front for world communization…the two communist regimes share the identical world communization goal and that free nations should pay serious attention to the possibility of Moscow Peiping rejoining for expansionist advances hand in hand…Free nations must abandon the mistaken and dangerous tactics of 'working with some communists in an attempt to check some others.'"[450] French Sinologist Jacques Guilleme Brulon noted in 1985 that: "*The present reforms as carried out by the Teng Hsiao-Ping Faction on the China Mainland is no more than the 'New Economic Policy' as having being introduced by Lenin when the Soviet Union faced immense difficulties in the 1920S…In fact, like the Soviet Union, Communist China is only utilizing the collaboration of the West to build up its strength in order to destroy the West eventually.*"[451]

During the process of open rapprochement between the Chinese and Soviet Communist Parties in 1989, columnist William Safire noted that "*For free nations, the Sino-Soviet rapprochement is not a net plus. We should stop smiling bravely and pretending that our hand is stronger without the China card in it.*" Safire also noted that this rapprochement would also help lead to a Korean re-unification under communist domination and would allow the Soviets to reallocate troops from the Far East to Eastern Europe to further threaten the NATO alliance. Safire concluded by stating: "*By all rational standards, the Sino-Soviet summit meeting is a historic advance for communist leaders in both countries and a setback for freedom -- unless it leads to communism's crack-up. Only in that unlikely case would it not be detrimental to our interests.*"[452]

Former Soviet economic advisor to Gorbachev and defector Yuri Maltsev noted in 1991 that "*The Soviet Union and China are now major allies because they are the only major communist regimes left in the world, apart from countries like Cuba and Albania. Mr. Bessmertnykh's (Foreign Minister) visit is very significant. I believe we will see relations between them going back to the close harmony they enjoyed before the great split of 1958…They have a lot in common.*" Former CIA official Herb Meyer noted that: "*They are natural allies; they need each other. They are the two lawless states left in the world. They've got nothing left now but one another.*" Former CIA Director and Defense Secretary noted James Schlesinger stated: "*The Soviets and Chinese are getting mutual comfort from their good relations. They live in a world that is more dominated by the United States than either of them are comfortable with. Neither government really approved of U.S. activities in the Gulf. It's a way of attempting to regain their influence.*"[453]

After the *"fall"* of the USSR in late December 1991, Sino-Russian relations experienced a continued expansion of military and economic contacts. This even reached into the realm of joint war planning and occupational strategies directed against the continental United States. According to a defecting GRU Colonel Stanislav Lunev, the Russian General Staff held a meeting in early 1992 in Moscow. According to Lunev, the Russian Generals "*were still committed to fighting and winning a future nuclear war against America. 'The nuclear war plan*

---

[450] "USSR, Red China Join Hands for World Communization, Dr. Ku Says" Central News Agency September 7, 1986

[451] "French Expert Warning West Against Naïve Policy Toward Peiping" Central News Agency – Taiwan April 3, 1985

[452] Safire, William "Sino-Soviet Friendship Not U.S. Plus" The Oregonian May 19, 1989 page B05

[453] Sieff, Martin "Events Re-link China, Soviets" Washington Times May 13, 1991 page A1

is still on,' he was told. But there would be changes. No longer would Russian troops be responsible for a follow-up invasion of the lower 48 states (U.S. mainland). Russian forces would be responsible for occupying 'Alaska and parts of Canada.' The Chinese would occupy the lower 48 states. In addition, certain Third World countries would be given 'looting rights.'"[454]

Chinese dictator Deng Xiaoping and Chen Yun issued reports that spoke of the cementing of Sino-Russian ties for the purpose of neutralizing American power: *"CCP issued two reports on the subject; Central Policy Research Centre report suggests 'a new relationship with Russia' to form a 'new strategy' against 'US hegemonism;' Military Research Office report suggests offering economic aid to Russia in exchange for sophisticated naval and air force equipment..."*

The CCP Central Policy Research Centre report noted that *"a stable and developing Russia promotes China's construction and reform, and will provide a peaceful and stable situation around us, something which US hegemonism opposes and hates to see. The report suggests that since Russia's economic reform has run into difficulty, China should provide whatever economic aid it can afford, including interest-free loans in renminbi ; low-interest, long-term loans in US dollars; help in light industrial, textile and food industries, labour, energy for development; and so on. China can sign long-term economic mutual accords, build an economic development and cooperation zone encompassing Russia, China, the CIS, Mongolia and South and North Korea."* This report also remarked that *"China and Russia should think in terms of generations of friendship between the two countries and the entire global strategic pattern, and sign a 'friendly, cooperative and nonaggression pact.'"* The Military Research Office Report 93017 supported *"Proposals to build a new type of friendly and cooperative relationship with Russia under the new international environment, points out that China should offer Russia economic aid, especially in light industry, food and meat in exchange for the purchase of Russian high, advanced and sophisticated naval and air force equipment, and strengthen exchanges and cooperation between Chinese and Russian scientists and military experts. The two countries should sign a defence and cooperation treaty under the new environment...Russia has a solid foundation in military, heavy and space industries, a large contingent of scientists and technologists, which overall is as strong as, if not stronger than, West European countries."*[455]

Cheng Ming reported in 1992 that the State Council Research Office and the Overseas Information Office called for the creation of *"an anti-American united front embracing China, North Korea and Vietnam, assisting the re-establishment of communist parties in the Soviet Union and Eastern Europe, supporting the Middle East countries' policies in opposition to the USA and the West, and wooing Third World countries to antagonize the USA."* One section of this foreign policy plan was titled *"Planning to Establish a China-North Korea-Vietnam United Front."* The text recommended that the Red Chinese should establish *"a united front embracing China, North Korea and Vietnam, and opposing the subversion, intervention, infiltration and aggression of the Third World by the West headed by US imperialism and assisting and allying with the peoples and political parties of the countries all over the world subjected to the bullying*

---

[454] Nyquist, J.R. "Chinese Paratroopers in California?" Accessed http://www.tldm.org/news4/chineseinvasion.htm

[455] "CCP Think-Tank Proposes a New Type of Relationship with Russia" Cheng Ming November 10, 1993

and oppression, exploitation and aggression by imperialism to resist the hegemony and power politics pursued by the countries headed by the USA. " Other specific points of the report called for "*Assisting the Re-establishment of Communist Parties in the Soviet Union and Eastern Europe; Giving moral support for and financial assistance to the re-establishment and restoration of Marxist political parties in Eastern Europe and the Soviet Union; Forming ties of allies based on mutual assistance with Pakistan and India and setting up an anti-aggression, anti-subversion joint military organ to contend with the USA; Supporting the Middle East countries' policies against the USA and the West, and supporting the countries in weakening the development of the Western economy by using petroleum as a weapon; Supporting the countries, political parties and organizations in Latin America in opposing US imperialist aggression, intervention, sabotage and subversion and giving material support to Cuba, which is an anti-American outpost.* " The report allegedly desired for China to increase its role as "*an anti-American, anti-imperialist centre.* '"[456]

There were reports that the KGB recruited the Chinese leadership of the 1990s back in the 1950s as agents of influence. It was reported that Jiang Zemin, Li Peng, and other Chinese CP leaders were trained in the USSR in the 1950s and were allegedly recruited by the KGB. It was reported that Jiang Zemin continued to correspond with his Soviet "*girlfriends*" through letters.[457] This could potentially point to the fact that the Chinese dictators during the 1990s and 2000s were *de facto* Soviet agents.

After the "*collapse*" of the USSR in December 1991, Moscow and Beijing greatly expanded their military cooperation. This cooperation included joint exercises between their military forces whose ultimate target was believed to be the United States. In 1992, the Russians supplied the PRC with 24 Su-27 fighter planes. Moscow also agreed to set up a production line at the Shenyang Aircraft Industry Company to produce Su-27s on Chinese territory. China also indicated interest in purchasing the Russian Su-35 and Su-37. In 1999, the Chinese purchased 60 Su-30 combat planes from Russia, thus spending $2 billion.[458]

In April 1996 Boris Yeltsin visited China and signed with Jiang Zemin a declaration announcing "*a long term strategic partnership.*" This partnership was no doubt targeted against the United States. By then, Russia supplied ICBMs, SU-27 aircraft, and Kilo class submarines to China along with thousands of Russian scientists and technicians who worked directly for Chinese military industries.[459]

In April 1997, Russian Defense Minister Igor Rodionov visited China to solidify military cooperation. Minister Rodinov noted in a meeting with PLA General Chi Haotian that "*Cooperation between the two armies is not aimed at a third country...but favours both regional and world security.*" In other words, the Russians and the Chinese were talking with the forked tongue. "*World security*" arguably is a code word for the neutralization of the United States as a superpower or even a great power and the ascendancy of Moscow and Beijing as the new

---

[456] "Hong Kong Paper on Chinese Conservatives Abortive Attempt to Form Front Against West" Cheng Ming April 4, 1992

[457] Pipko, Simona. The Russian Factor (eBookIt.com, 2011) Chapter 6

[458] "Russian Purchases Boost China's Air Strength" Yazhou Zhoukan August 28, 1999.

[459] Munro, Ross H. and Bernstein, Richard. The Coming Conflict With China (Vintage Books, 1998) page 47.

dominant powers. General Chi reported that China and Russia would continue to *"maintain and develop relations between the two armies, but bilateral relations globally."*[460]

In 1999, China bought 40 Russian Su-30 fighter-bombers worth about $2 billion. The Chinese also purchased 76 Su-27s, four Kilo class submarines, and six S-300 air defense systems that could shoot down short range missiles.[461]

Cooperation extended on the level of strategic nuclear war planning against the United States by the dawn of the Twenty First Century. In 2001, Russian troops joined in a Chinese PLA nuclear attack exercise conducted against the United States for assistance rendered to Taiwan. The exercises involved strategic bombing runs conducted by Russian Air Force Tu-22 and Su-27 planes near Japan. The Tu-22s were equipped with nuclear cruise missiles. The Sino-Russian exercise carried this sequence of events: *"The Asia scenario began with a Chinese military attack on Taiwan that was followed by the use of U.S. ground troops on the island, said one official. Next, China escalated the conflict by firing tactical nuclear missiles on the U.S. troops in Taiwan, prompting U.S. nuclear strikes on Chinese forces. Russian nuclear forces then threatened to use nuclear missile strikes on U.S. forces in the region, including strikes on troops in South Korea and Japan."* Russia also fired ICBMs from land launchers and SLBMs from submarines during this particular exercise.[462]

In August 2005, another Sino-Russian military exercise was conducted called *"Peace Mission 2005."* The exercise will take place in Vladivostok, Russia, and on the Shandong Peninsula and nearby waters in China. Ten thousand army, navy, air force, marines, and support personnel were involved in "*Peace Mission 2005.*" The Hong Kong news agency Zhongguo Tongxun She noted that "*Russian Army Deputy Commander Moltenskoy indicated on the 2nd that the Russian army will sent 1,800 officers and soldiers to participate in the joint military exercise. Participating Russian units include the Russian Pacific Fleet's large antisubmarine vessel Marshal Shaposhnikov, a large amphibious landing ship, a destroyer, and a company of marines, as well as 17 long-range military transport planes and fighter planes and one company of the Pskov 76th Airborne Division...Participating Chinese and Russian forces will move to China's Jiaodong Peninsula and an area of the Yellow Sea. According to the scenario, a company of Russian paratroops will board transport planes and execute an airborne landing somewhere on the Jiaodong Peninsula, directly 'into the enemy's rear area,' in coordination with units of the Chinese army, navy, and air force. Meanwhile, a company of Russian marines will board a large amphibious landing ship and seize a beachhead in a sea area on the Jiaodong Peninsula. Phase three of the exercise will begin on 23 August. Russian frontline air forces will mobilize an Su-27SM fighter element to provide cover for two Russian long-range air forces Tu-95MS 'Bear' strategic bombers and four Tu-22M3 'Backfire' long-range bombers as they fly over the Yellow Sea and use cruise missiles to attack targets on the sea surface. Because of misgivings on the part of certain countries about this joint military exercise, Russian Defence Minister Ivanov, who is in Vladivostok to inspect, indicated the other day that no third country*

---

[460] Hewitt, Giles. "Russian defence minister defends arms sales to China" Agence France Presse April 15, 1997

[461] Gertz, Bill and Scarborough, Rowan. "Inside the Ring Russia-China Ties" Washington Times September 3, 1999 page A6.

[462] Gertz, Bill. "Russian Forces Help China in Mock Conflict; Nuclear War on U.S. Troops" Washington Times April 30, 2001 page A1

has any reason whatsoever to worry about the joint military exercise which Russia and China will conduct in August. Russia and China are neighbours and strategic partners."[463]

A US official noted that *"For the Chinese and the Russians, this is a message to the United States. They want to see our bases in Central Asia and presence in Asia cut back."*[464]

During his visit to Red China, Putin supported the *"comprehensive strategic partnership"* between both nations. Russian Foreign Minister Lavrov noted that *"Russia and China have common core interests. They hold similar stances on the ongoing profound changes in the world and similar approaches to new challenges."*[465]

The Red Chinese and Russian Navies conducted five days of joint live-fire military exercises codenamed *"Maritime Cooperation-2012"* in the Yellow Sea. The joint exercises focused on submarine and airborne threats.[466]

The United Russia Party leaders convened a special meeting to explore how they could emulate the Chinese Communist Party on financial and economic issues. Deputy Prime Minister and senior Putin aide Aleksandr D. Zhukov noted *"The accomplishments of China's Communist Party in developing its government deserve the highest marks."*[467]

In July 2009, ITAR-TASS reported that *"Russian troops are getting aboard a Chinese train Wednesday to take part in joint anti-terrorist exercises Peace Mission 2009, that will be held on the Chinese territory."* Troops who participated in this exercise included a Russian motorized rifle battalion and airborne company. The Red Chinese transported 150 Russian tanks, armored personnel carriers, and trucks. At least 20 Russian bombers, fighter jets, transports, and helicopters also participated in the Peace Mission 2009 exercise.[468]

In conclusion, it is quite clear that the feigned *"independence"* of Romania in the 1960s and 1970s was a calculated deception to fool the West and the United States into increasing the transfer of high technology items and the provision of trade privileges to Bucharest. Furthermore, the Soviets and the Romanians would also gain the added strategic advantage of misinforming the West and the Americans into viewing the communist empire as less than monolithic and therefore of little threat to the Free World. It is important to realize that even if the Soviet *"splits"* with Albania and China were *bona fide,* the two countries were still aligned with Moscow's desire to overtake and destroy the independence and freedom in the United States. The evidence that I put forth in this paper clearly illustrates this point. Also, the historical facts also confirm that Albania and China healed their *"splits"* with the Soviet Union and

---

[463] Hui, Yang. "Hong Kong Agency Gives Details of China-Russia Military Exercise" <u>Zhongguo Tongxun</u> She August 2, 2005

[464] Gertz, Bill. "War Games Seen As 'Message;' China-Russia Military Exercises Worry U.S. Officials" <u>Washington Times</u> August 17, 2005 page A01

[465] Eisenman, Joshua. "Taiwan opposition seeks new leader; Russia and China celebrate relations 'at an all time high'" <u>China Reform Monitor</u> June 25, 2012 Accessed From: http://www.afpc.org/publication_listings/viewBulletin/1584

[466] "China and Russia Hold Joint Large Scale Naval Exercises" <u>China Reform Monitor</u> May 11, 2012 Accessed From: http://www.freerepublic.com/focus/f-news/2882876/posts

[467] Levy, Clifford J. "Russia's Leaders See China as Template for Ruling" <u>New York Times</u> October 17, 2009 Accessed From: http://www.freerepublic.com/focus/news/2365109/posts

[468] Jasper, William F. "Decades of Suicidal Policies Vis-à-vis Russia and China" <u>The New American</u> July 22, 2009 Accessed From: http://www.thenewamerican.com/world-news/europe/item/8452-decades-of-suicidal-policies-vis-%C3%A0-vis-russia-and-china

subsequently deepened their relations with Moscow. The renewed alliance of Beijing with Moscow deepened in the 1990s and 2000s, much to the detriment of the long term power and independence of the United States. Meanwhile, American big business and their globalist enablers in the political class, lobbyists, and establishment think tanks turn a blind eye or even enable the growing superpowers in Russia and Red China. It is imperative that we recognize that *"splits"* in the totalitarian blocs of power-whether Islamist or Communist/Great Russian Nationalist-Leninism-are ploys to misinform the United States regarding the scope of the threat to forces that mortally threaten the lives and existence of the United States and its people.

CPSIA information can be obtained
at www.ICGtesting.com
Printed in the USA
LVHW022307020919

629681LV00008B/343/P

9 781514 238974